†

AN EXPERIENTIAL APPROACH TO SPIRITUAL FORMATION

GREG ROBINSON, PhD

Published by:

Wood 'N' Barnes Publishing & Distribution
2309 N. Willow, Suite A
Bethany, Oklahoma 73008
405-942-6812
800-678-0621
woodnbarnes.com

God is a being that is beyond one gender or the other. Yet, there is a limitation in the English language in that we do not have words that can reflect this truth. So, in this book, I have chosen to use the traditional use of masculine language to speak of God.

Cover Design by Blue Designs
Copyediting & Design by Ramona Cunningham

Printed in the United States of America
Oklahoma City, Oklahoma
ISBN # 978-1-885473-81-3

In memory of my mom, who let me experience unconditional acceptance every day of my life.

Content

Which questions guide our lives?
Which questions do we make our own?
Which questions deserve our undivided attention and full personal commitment?
Finding the right questions is as crucial as finding the right answers.

—Henri Nouwen

• Foreword

Depending on where you sat each Sunday morning at 10:00 a.m. during your formative years, you'll have a different take on this book. If, like me, you were sitting in Sunday School, then this book will be a welcome relief from the idea that spiritual formation consists primarily of instruction about how to conduct oneself—the "what" questions of life. If you weren't steeped in a tradition that offered instruction on dos and don'ts, then this book will reassure you that some very thoughtful followers of Jesus are doing new work that goes deeper to the "why" and "how" questions that actually form the foundation of our "what."

In taking up the topic of spiritual formation and its facilitation, Greg addresses an area that is often considered to be the opposite of the freewheeling ethos of experiential learning. This is precisely why we need this book. Instead of offering up another frozen TV dinner that only needs 5 minutes in the microwave before it spits out hot, steaming instruction-manual-like solutions for our life's problems, Greg steps back. Way back. And reintroduces us to the concept of a kitchen, and food, and something called "cooking."

Drawing on his substantial experience as a facilitator of change, Greg applies time-tested principles of personal development to his topic of spiritual growth. After several warnings against attempts to replicate his particular path, he lovingly peppers the book with honest personal reflections that demonstrate his willingness to live the question himself before introducing it to others. Inviting us to "risk the unfamiliar," Greg takes us down a path that, for some, might appear dangerous at first—the idea of questioning God, setting adrift from some of our pat answers, and seeing what happens when we ask the questions we are most afraid of asking. A journey that, in my mind, is likely to be rewarded, and one that almost certainly will result in growth.

Leading off with a quote about "selling our souls to the grade-givers," we quickly get a picture of where our author thinks the journey will lead. If that quote excites you, read this book. If that quote offends you, read this book. Greg lovingly and thoughtfully lays out the case for an intrinsic faith that is grounded in personal experience and authenticity. This is not another rant about toxic churches or dangerous pastors. Rather, it reads like a fireside chat with a loving, wise grandparent who wants nothing more than for us to live out the rest of our days free from the tyranny of blame, external validation, and fear. Greg masterfully helps us travel well on our spiritual path, without telling us exactly where to go—the holy grail of experiential learning, and evidence of years spent honing his skills.

May this fireside chat lead you and those you influence into the journey of a lifetime.

¡Adelante!

Mark Regouby, MTS
Harvard Divinity School (with coursework at the Fletcher School of Law and Diplomacy and the Harvard Kennedy School), Founder of PersonalPhilanthropy.org and Cofounder of TellTheirStory.org, Member of the Committee on Women, Gender, and Sexuality in Religion, Harvard Divinity School (2008-2009).

Preface

As I looked behind me, I could see the top of the oak tree from which the long and slender platform extended shake and twist with every move I made. Looking forward, I could see the bottom of the ravine way below where it appeared the open maul of the earth was ready to swallow me. I heard the metal clink as the carabiner gate closed into place. Immediately it hit me, the weight of the cables pulling me toward the edge. The harder I resisted, the greater the tension on the swing cables and the stronger the draw to the edge. I was faced with a decision at that point in time. On one hand, I could allow my fear to keep me frozen in place. Although the status quo was unpleasant and unsustainable, I knew what I had there on the end of that platform. The other choice was to keep resisting the source of my fear and let the weight of the cables do their job and pull me into the unknown, where after a second or two of weightless uncertainty, I would experience the adventure of a lifetime. I am glad I took the leap.

This same scenario could be a description of my life of faith. I have had different sources of fear that motivated me toward God. At first it was the fear of judgment and punishment. I am glad that God had something much better in mind. My experiences, both structured and planned as well as those happenstances of life, have continued to question the skewed vision I had of God. Each time I was willing to question what I thought I knew, I discovered a clearer picture of the truth.

Now I want to ask you to take the same leap. There is more to faith than the legal image of a God that requires justice. That is our image: the one we have clung to in order to make up for our lack of trust. The legal God we can understand and deal with because

> Each time I was willing to question what I thought I knew, I discovered a clearer picture of the truth.

that God is so much like us. The God we have forgotten existed in friendship with us before the great "Fall" in the Garden of Eden. That God came and walked among us. That God has chosen since the foundation of the earth to reconcile with us at all costs. The journey to see beyond the religious image of the legal God will require us to gain new practices, ideas, and equipment to unlearn our illusions and relearn a clearer understanding of the truth. For that we will need more than information, rules, and programs. We will need experience, community, and an adventurous curiosity that will keep asking questions and trusting things like reflection, solitude, and authenticity to change our lives and, in the end, the world.

Consequently, our journey together will start with understanding those images of God and the end result that we believe a life of faith is drawing us toward. For the spiritual facilitator, this will begin with exploring your personal beliefs as a practice field for preparing to help others do the same. Once we have a better understanding of the destination God's adventure is calling us toward, we will turn our attention to how we can create space and time for others to encounter their own illusions and learn a different kind of faith.

My hope is that those who read this book will begin to ask a new and different set of questions about the work of faith building and spiritual formation, which will in turn stimulate you to create new ways of doing the work you are already doing. In fact, let me ask a few right now to see if they connect with where you are:

Would you dare to consider a spirituality that is not dependent upon being right, good, and productive?

If you could see a way to understand your true identity, would you dare to look?

If it were possible to foster authentic community made up of the mature and the curious, would you dare to try?

If you answered yes to any of these questions, then open these pages and consider an experiential approach to spiritual formation. In the practices of retreat, pilgrimage, and service lies the adventurous journey of discovering who we are and how we can live well in the world we have been given. As the poet Robert Frost once wrote, "Two roads diverged in a wood, and I—I took the one less traveled by, and that has made all the difference." Will you consider such a journey?

Think for Yourself

Stretch your imagination and open your mind as you consider how to work differently with those who are trying to grow their faith. I am not offering a ready-made plan. I will ask more questions than give answers. The goal is for you, the reader, to begin to think differently about what you do and how you do it. I believe all work that is truly effective in growing our spirits is local and particular. Local in that it will happen in a specific place and time. Particular in that it will happen with a particular set of people, with a particular set of stories, trials, and issues, with a particular leader who has his or her own unique story. I cannot and would not presume to say how you will do this work with others. But I can ask some provocative questions and tell you something about the answers I have unearthed with the intent of helping you to begin thinking for yourself and starting your own path rather than replicating mine.

What is an Adventurous Discipleship?

Discipleship is a term that describes a very intentional, purposeful, and disciplined effort to learn a particular set of teachings and live a particular way of life. In the Christian church it is used to describe the chosen path to understand and follow the way of Jesus. It is this particular work that this book is most dedicated to. That is not to say that only followers of Jesus will learn from the book. There are many kinds of lessons that can be found in the discussion that follows.

> The kind of relationship that God wants from us is one that we live into as we dare to trust in the acceptance He has offered.

Adventure is something where the outcome is not predetermined nor controlled by us. Too much of contemporary Christianity is embedded in a system of thought that focuses on what we can do, understand, and control. According to this perspective, faith is a contract to be honored. The signs of success involve being right, good, and productive. Alternatively, the faith that we are invited into with Jesus is as unpredictable as the lives we live. So an adventurous discipleship is a way of understanding Jesus' message and life that calls us deeper into the mystery of love and trust. As a result of answering this call, we realize that things have been set right with God and that our true value is defined by His actions for us. The kind of relationship that God wants from us cannot be found in talking about God. It is a relationship that we live into as we dare to trust in the acceptance He has offered.

A Common Language

To keep us on the same page (so to speak), the definitions of some of the terms you will encounter in this book follow. The foundation of good conversation is common language, and I want to make sure we share one.

Spiritual Formation: According to Henri Nouwen (2006), spiritual formation is the ongoing process of learning to trust who God says that I am. It is a lifelong process of learning to hear the right voice, the one that reminds me I am beloved and accepted by God. It is also an ongoing struggle to silence, or at least recognize those voices that would have me question the truth of my standing with God. As we will see in the next chapter, spiritual formation is God's action in my life that will allow me to grow up and enter into an authentic relationship with God and others.

Spiritual Facilitator: a person who comes alongside of others to help them find their way as they allow God to grow their faith.

Adventure: something where the outcome is not predetermined nor controlled by us.

Discipleship: a very intentional, purposeful, and disciplined effort to learn a particular set of teachings and live a particular way of life.

Containers: a defined place, time frame, or process that is set aside to learn and discover new ideas, skills, and attitudes.

Processing: purposeful reflection on an experience with the intent of distilling meaningful lessons contained in that experience. It also involves connecting lessons from a particular experience to other parts of our lives outside that experience or activity.

Belay Systems: the equipment that keeps climbers safe as they participate in some adventure activities like rock climbing or ropes courses, generally including a strong anchor, ropes, friction devices, and pulleys.

One of the best contexts for discovery is experiential learning. This is a type of learning that requires action, reflection, and an undetermined result. In a word, spiritual formation requires adventure.

—Greg Robinson

Introduction

Two roads diverged in a wood, and I—
I took the one less traveled by,
And that has made all the difference.
—Robert Frost

Nearly 20 years ago now, I was 60 feet up an 80-foot cliff. I found myself paralyzed by fear and uncertainty. The person on the end of my rope was a 19 year old who had never before rock climbed. Although I knew the equipment would work and keep me safe, I did not have the same assurances about him. Running out of strength, my mind clouded, and I could not find a way forward. In the next moment, I fell. The rope held, as did my belayer, and I quickly completed the climb with little effort.

Looking back I see in this short encounter the essence of my experience on Frost's "road less traveled." You see, for me, going down the less-traveled path has been more about simple choices and less about some spectacular scenario. These choices were around moments when I could have stayed trapped in the known or risked the unfamiliar; I was compelled to choose the unknown. When I started thinking for myself in high school rather than letting teachers tell me what to do—when I started asking the tough questions about the faith and doctrine that had been programmed into me as a child—these were the points in time where my life's path was determined.

I realized after falling on my climb that my fear was perceived rather than real. When I started listening to the restlessness, dissatisfaction, and inconsistency in my set of beliefs about God and began asking different questions, I found that the fear I had about questioning what I thought was truth was more perceived fear rather than real fear. I discovered that God was not afraid of my questions. In fact, He was calling me into those questions.

I discovered that God was not afraid of my questions. In fact, He was calling me into those questions.

For me, the "road less traveled" has led to a chance at life beyond fear. The lessons I heard and believed when I was young made me jealous, afraid, critical, and distant, just like the God I was taught I had to serve. What I have discovered is freedom and peace that do not depend on my performance but are found in the assurance of my acceptance by God. For the first time, I have started liking myself, not fearing other people, and experiencing something of the deeper mystery of God's actions for humanity.

This book is my update on the adventurous journey that Robert Frost entices us with. More explicitly, it is a set of thoughts to help those who are in a position to help, teach, lead, or mentor others who are at their own crossroads, wondering if the lonely less-traveled road is for them. I invite you to read slowly and listen closely as you join me in thinking about our part in God's work on earth.

The essence of this book is reflected in this quote by Henri Nouwen (1988), "Which questions guide our lives? Which questions do we make our own? Which questions deserve our undivided attention and full personal commitment? Finding the right questions is as crucial as finding the right answers" (p. 25). For me, the path to life has been completely about the questions I ask. Will you dare such adventurous curiosity yourself?

The Intent of the Facilitation

This book addresses three critical questions for those seeking to create lasting and sustainable change. The first of those questions is, "What is the intent or end toward which I work?" For too long, the priority of the church has been morality. There is nothing wrong with teaching and encouraging a moral life. The problem is that we miss the mark when we come to believe that morality is the means to spiritual life rather than the by-product of a spiritual life. At one time I led a group on Sunday nights. As we struggled together to understand how to grow in our experience and trust of God, one of our members asked the question that I have found so often on the lips of those seeking spiritual life. "So are you saying," he said, "that the more I love God the better person I will become?" My response was, "No, the more we let God love us, the better people we will become." This highlights why it is so important to reflect on and understand the intent of our ministry. When we see morality as the means to spiritual life, we put the wrong person at the center of

What is the intent or end toward which I work?

the story. We put ourselves in the center and God on the periphery. I believe we need to learn to put God at the center and ourselves at the periphery.

In fact, the reason we are focused on morality is that Western Christianity has been focused on the wrong part of the story. Most of the history of Western Christianity has focused on the fall in the garden (Genesis 3) and the legal requirements to fix that failure. In fact, "the anxiety and insecurity and guilt" (Kruger, 2003) experienced after the fall continues to skew our understanding of God.

> *From this moment forward, the truth about God will be veiled, His face will be continually tarred with the wrong brush, and His heart will be misunderstood. His every word and act and intention will be translated through the wrongheadedness of human anxiety and projection. The very presence of God in love and grace and fellowship will be translated through the fallen mind as the presence of one whose love is arbitrary and hinges on conditions, whose blessing comes with strings attached, if it comes at all, and whose character is chiefly that of a judge* (Kruger, 2003, p. 27).

If we are to hope to recover the community of God's intention we must remember the part of the story we have forgotten. Before the fall, God walked with Adam and Eve in the cool of the day (Genesis 3:8). Before the fall, God created human beings to join the Father, Son, and Holy Spirit in complete freedom and acceptance of the relationship they have with each other. The reconciliation of that once-experienced relationship is the central story line of history. "From the beginning, God is Father, Son, and Spirit, and from the beginning, this God has determined not to exist without us" (Kruger, p. 54). The remembering of this story will change forever the nature of the communities we create and live in.

> It is no longer our accomplishments, but God's action that tells us we are acceptable.

There is an alternative intent offered by Jesus, his disciple John, and the apostle Paul—a maturity rooted in a new identity. As followers of Christ we come to see ourselves defined by God's action for us rather than by our own actions. We come to trust the grace given to us, and our understanding of what makes us valuable. It is no longer our accomplishments, but God's action that tells us we are acceptable. Though it may be possible to articulate these ideas, it is a very different thing to live consistently by this truth. And though we may dare to hope this is true about ourselves, the ability to see it as true in others, in spite of their actions toward us, is troublesome work. The intent of our discipleship effort is to create a mature and thoughtful person, whose sense of worth is rooted deeply in the grace and mercy of God's acts.

The Facilitator's Equipment

The second question this book seeks to answer is, "What things are best suited to help others grow spiritually, and what equipment is at the disposal of the spiritual facilitator?" The work of spiritual nurture is not typical work. You cannot always come at it head on. Much of what limits us spiritually is rooted in ideas and patterns of response that lie beneath awareness. For this reason, much of what we need to learn must be discovered. The discovery, however, will create a good deal of turmoil in our lives until we are reoriented in our ways of thinking and living. Spiritual facilitators help others through their own presence, the conditions they create and maintain, and the effective use of questions to point, nudge, direct, and teach those who want to learn. One of the best contexts for discovery is experiential learning. This is a type of learning that requires action, reflection, and an undetermined result. In a word, spiritual formation requires adventure.

WHAT HELPS OTHERS GROW SPIRITUALLY, AND WHAT EQUIPMENT IS AT THE DISPOSAL OF THE SPIRITUAL FACILITATOR?

I would like to clarify something about this equipment. Although a clear description of each will be included in the following pages, the manifestation or use of these tools can come in a multitude of places and formats. There is no single best way to affect the life of another. The truth is that the previously mentioned tools will help us influence others, whether they are used in a classroom setting, a trip, a structured experience, or a happenstance event in life. The bottom line is that who you are as a leader/facilitator is more important than what you do. So my hope is that your imagination and God's providence will lead you to use these tools in very individual ways.

THE BOTTOM LINE IS THAT WHO YOU ARE AS A FACILITATOR IS MORE IMPORTANT THAN WHAT YOU DO.

Barriers to the Spiritual Quest

> What are the issues that we work to reveal and overcome?

The third and final question of this inquiry is, "What are the issues that we work to reveal and overcome?" Though there are many manifestations of limitations that stand in the way of our truly accepting and living in our acceptance by God, there are three that stand out. Two of the three empower or direct all the others; the third is the collective outcome of the other two.

The first issue that we must assault is **fear**. "The core message of all the great spiritual traditions is 'Be not afraid'" (Palmer, 1990). These are the first words of nearly all human encounters with the Divine in the Bible. Fear is at the root of all that turns us from the path of God. We are afraid of not measuring up. We are afraid of a God who is so great. We are afraid we do not have what we need for life. If we do not find ways to mitigate our fear, it will consume us, leaving us as lifeless bodies just passing the time or living on the edge hoping to find something greater than our fear to possess us. In the still, soft whisper of our God, we hear, "Be not afraid." How do we live with less fear?

The second core issue is related to the first. Fear causes us to **doubt**, and we doubt no one more quickly than God. If we look deeply at our misdeeds and wrong behavior, we find mistrust at their roots. We do not trust in the deal God has made. How can those who do not deserve, and for the most part do not consciously desire reconciliation and pardon, receive it freely nonetheless? But this is exactly what the Bible tells us. We have been set right (Col. 1:19-23). Our value and acceptance by God is assured. We must come to trust it. The central work is to set aside our fear and recognize how our mistrust too often guides our actions and defines our identity. This is a lifelong endeavor, for there are many ways that fear and mistrust influence us. We may awake in a moment of repentance, but it will take a lifetime of attention to bring hope and love to the forefront of our lives. How do we make this journey?

> If we are to relearn seeing God among us, we must find something other than success and affluence to motivate our actions.

The third issue is the **collective consequence of a fearful people**. When we are not sure of our standing, we often turn toward our productivity to supplant our lack of faith. We live in a culture that is driven by ambition, but it is an ambition born of fear. How can I secure my place? I can produce. I can be relevant. I can build, control, and direct. Even our churches have been influenced by this ambition. If we are to relearn seeing God moving among us, we must find something other than success and affluence to motivate our actions. The collective expression of the gospel is community. John, in his first letter, gives us a picture of what our community can become. We will explore in some depth the alternative to ambition that the church is called to embody. Without an observable alternative, the world will never consider that something other than ambition could motivate our dreams.

An Overview of Our Journey

The aim of the first half of this book is to awaken our imagination concerning both a goal or purpose toward which to work and the means which we use to do our work. This journey begins in Chapter 1 by looking at what we are trying to do when helping others develop their faith. The destination you are striving to reach will determine not only the path you are taking but also how you will travel along that path. For instance, if you believe your job is to get the right answers into a person's mind, then your means and methods will focus on communicating good information, providing rebuttals when your answers are questioned, and limiting the kinds of questions that a person may ask in the first place. If, however, you want to help a person mature and develop a deeper understanding of his or her identity, then you have to use methods that promote discovery and broaden the set of questions that a person may ask.

Chapter 2 explores the unique domain of adventure as a way to help facilitate spiritual formation. To understand our identities, we must contact our fears, wrestle with limitations, and challenge our assumptions. Adventure—experiences where the outcome is not predetermined—is an ideal space for real faith to develop. This chapter defines adventure and why it works as a learning medium.

Chapter 3 continues the discussion of our goal or destination with a focus on understanding the hurdles and barriers that not only keep us from knowing who we really are but also keep us from living true to our identities. These are the challenges that we must help others prepare for so they don't abandon their faith journey altogether.

Chapter 4 provides a map of sorts to understanding how people learn and change their identities. The dynamics of change can either empower us to grow or continue to sidetrack us. A way of thinking about and making sense of this type of deep learning places you in a better position to assess and assist others who are in process.

Although the path of faith and spiritual formation is personal, it cannot be accomplished alone. It is also true that not every community is equally equipped to help us pursue spiritual formation. Consequently, Chapter 5 takes a look at John's first epistle to see what it can tell us of the type of Christian community that can help a genuine, authentic faith grow. This chapter also provides some signposts to help you determine if you are moving in the right direction with your groups.

As you might suspect at this point, since we are pursuing a new destination in our faith work, we will need a particular set of methods to help us. Chapters 6 and 7 explore a way of teaching that moves beyond providing predetermined answers. These chapters look at facilitation, an approach to teaching that is primarily concerned with creating the conditions that will enable people to grow and learn.

Chapter 8 outlines three containers that provide environments for spiritual formation. A container is a defined experience with a particular set of values and goals where we become aware of certain things and practice changes we would like to make in our thinking, feelings, and actions. A container includes a specific location, time, and space designed to engage us with questions and experiences that we do not notice or have on our own.

Chapter 9 describes some of the forms these containers have taken in my work with others. Sometimes the containers appeared as events or trips, other times as processes or programs. This chapter is written with the hope that your imagination will be stirred to consider different ways to help others learn.

We conclude this journey in Chapters 10 and 11, discussing how to create a strategy that utilizes purposeful experience in a thoughtful and effective way. Chapter 10 includes a set of reflection questions for assessing your own ideas and developing new, more effective approaches. Chapter 11 is not just a "how-to" chapter with a checklist for running a good retreat. It is a model that will help you consider how to prepare a person for different and deeper experiences of life with God.

When we start being too impressed by the results of our work, we slowly come to the erroneous conviction that life is one large scoreboard where someone is listing the points to measure our worth. And before we are fully aware of it, we have sold our souls to the grade-givers.

—Henri Nouwen

1 What Is the Intent or End Toward Which I Work?

The sand and water was much warmer than the chilled air suggested as we stepped onto the pilgrims' path, the ancient route across the sands during low tide. In front of us was our final destination—the Holy Island of Lindisfarne. The guide poles stretched out in front of us marking the final 2 miles of this week-long walk. Our last hour of this pilgrimage seemed a perfect combination of its parallel journey that is my life. What at times was a clear and compelling direction disappeared in a moment as the island became wrapped in the storm that was bearing down on us. Only the marking poles gave a sense of direction, otherwise we would be lost.

The same has been true in trying to understand faith and God and my place in the Divine story. I want to invite you to join me for a while. I am going to ask you to entertain some questions that may create moments of uncertainty and fog. Although the overall purpose of this book is to describe a way of helping others find their way on their own life adventure, we must consider the assumptions and beliefs that make us who we are. For it is who we are, who we believe ourselves to be, that will make all the difference. The methods described are just excuses to interact, ways to engage others. They can be used to promote dead religion or awaken others to the grand narrative of God's choice of reconciliation with us. The identity and beliefs of the facilitator determine which turn will be taken.

I have experienced two ways of thinking about the spiritual life. One works well as long as we are successful, have a good public image, and do not ask too many questions. The other works only for those who are broken and defeated. The former led me to judge others, argue and debate others, classify others, and in the secret places of my heart, envy those who were not so burdened with the rules I was struggling to keep.

On the surface, the message I grew up with, as did many who have been active in evangelical churches, seems good. Study God and His Word, be clear on the answers to life's temptations, do good things, and stop doing bad things. Help others see the light whatever the cost. The dark side of this message is that it caused me to grow angry, self-righteous, guilty, and afraid. It moved my efforts to be good to the center of the story and God's work for me to the periphery. It did cause me to work hard, be very active in the church, and study diligently. Yet at the end of the day, I no more experienced God than the atheist next door. I had no spiritual vitality and nothing but image and empty words to offer.

The second way of thinking, "for the least, the lost, the little, and the dead" (Capon, 1998) comes with a much less glamorous message. I learned it from people who had been through the dark night and emerged to live on the other side. Lest we romanticize their struggle, they too often suffered because of their own decisions, their own fears, and their own leanings toward the darkness. I will introduce you to some of them because you will need to know people like this. Only people who have suffered to the point that they have less fear of asking the questions that we typically don't ask can help us see other possibilities. Only those who have been humbled and lost belief in their own success will dare to speak of another way to understand the life and message of Jesus.

ONLY PEOPLE WHO HAVE SUFFERED TO THE POINT THAT THEY HAVE LESS FEAR OF ASKING QUESTIONS CAN HELP US SEE OTHER POSSIBILITIES.

The intent that interests me results in people who would rather do good than bad, but they do what they do based on very different motivations. Growing up spiritually, experiencing and trusting the gift of grace, and learning to see ourselves as Jesus sees us requires that we learn to hold tight to different things—different priorities, different responses to those unlike us, and a very different vision of the spiritual community of the church. Here are some lessons I am learning while reforming my own vision of where I should be heading in my life and ministry.

Identity

"Spirituality means waking up. Most people, even though they don't know it, are asleep. They're born asleep, they live asleep, they marry in their sleep... they die in their sleep without ever waking up" (de Mello, 1990, p. 5). Ultimately, I believe this is the critical role of the spiritual facilitator. By asking important questions, we can help people begin to ask themselves the questions that will wake them up. These questions begin with, "Who am I?" and "What makes me important and valuable?" Ultimately these are the questions that are the foundation of our identity, our sense of self.

By asking important questions, we can help people begin to ask themselves the questions that will wake them up.

The apostle Paul returns to this idea repeatedly in his writing. "Don't copy the behaviors and customs of this world, but let God transform you into a new person by *changing the way you think*" [italics added] (Romans 12:2). We cannot stop and just focus on behaviors. Our actions are the logical outcomes of how we think, the assumptions that we make, and the way we see ourselves, others, God, and the world. The fact is that if we do not really understand this point, we will take behaviors that are meant for good, things that are designed to help us succeed and grow, and turn them into things that lead us away from God and thus farther away from who we are made to be.

> *When we start being too impressed by the results of our work, we slowly come to the erroneous conviction that life is one large scoreboard where someone is listing the points to measure our worth. And before we are fully aware of it, we have sold our souls to the grade-givers. That means we are not only*

in the world but also of the world. Then we become what the world makes us. We are intelligent because someone gives us a high grade. We are helpful because someone says thanks. We are likable because someone likes us. And we are important because someone considers us indispensable. In short, we are worthwhile because we have successes (Nouwen, 1974, p. 18-19).

This principle is just as true for good works, good rule-keeping—in short, morality—as it is for achievements and accomplishments. Too many people, myself included, have heard a message from the church that we are worthwhile only if we change to meet the church's expectations of a good Christian. If you doubt this, ask yourself if you believe God loves people just as much if they never change. Even though we've been given Paul's description of grace in chapter 2 of Ephesians, we still require people at some point to be different and that difference needs to align with our view of what "right" is. Do we really trust that people who really experience the unconditional grace and acceptance of God will become who they were made to become? Our intentions are good. We want to make sure that people act on the faith they have been given. However, we too often believe the end justifies the means; we start working toward compliance with a particular behavioral profile, so that we can easily detect who is with us and who is against us. I will say it again: Morality is the by-product of someone who knows God's grace and has experienced God's presence, not the path to that grace, to that presence, or to the spiritual life.

Do we really trust that people who really experience the unconditional grace and acceptance of God will become who they were made to become?

Now, if this new identity is to grow in us, we must understand who God sees us to be. And to be true to Scripture, we must realize that this identity is in no way a result of anything we do. We cannot do enough good or avoid enough bad. Who we are is determined by and defined by God's action.

Long ago, even before he made the world, God loved us and chose us in Christ to be holy and without fault in his eyes (Ephesians 1:4).

For God in all his fullness was pleased to live in Christ, and by him God reconciled everything to himself. He made peace with everything in heaven and on earth by means of his blood on the cross. This includes you who were once so far away from God. You were his enemies, separated from him by your evil thoughts and actions, yet now he has brought you back as his friends... As a result, he has brought you into the very presence of God and you are holy and blameless as you stand before him without a single fault. But you must continue to believe this truth and stand in it firmly (COLOSSIANS 2:19-23).

We are accepted completely by God. And the real mystery of this is that it has always been that way. He has always accepted us. Our struggle as humans is that we find it very difficult to believe this. I know I believed this to be true, to a point. Yet, as I looked within, I began to awaken to the fact that I did what I did most of the time to prove myself worthy, or to pay God back for His great sacrifice, or because I doubted that just believing in His acceptance would be enough to make my life full.

> MY SENSE OF VALUE DOES NOT REQUIRE THE VALIDATION OF OTHERS BUT IS FOUNDED ON THE TRUST THAT GOD'S ACTIONS ON MY BEHALF MAKE ME "GOOD ENOUGH."

God has made peace with us. We are His friends. For me to mature spiritually, this must be the foundation of my identity. This is what tells me who I am. This is true for everyone, according to Paul, but most of us never wake to this realization. The outcome for me has been that I am much less fearful, much less judgmental, and much more capable of seeing people for who they are, rather than what they choose to present to me. This is the beginning of the spiritual life.

Before we move beyond identity, there is one more aspect of this we must understand. Just because God sees me a certain way does not mean that I am formed by that perception. I must come to own my identity for myself. I cannot believe because my parents believe, my pastor or priest believes, or even my church believes. I must believe for myself. I must own it regardless of what the environment tells me. This is maturity. This is growing up. If I am successful, my sense of value will not require the validation of others but will be founded on the trust that God's actions on my behalf make me "good enough."

Practical Implications for Spiritual Facilitators: There are some practical implications of this idea of identity for all who would be spiritual facilitators. First, I can act as a guide who has made some progress. I can support you on your way, but I cannot choose your way for you. I cannot make my path your path. Consequently, the best assistance I can provide is to bring others to the point of crossroad decisions and see what choices they make. Secondly, waking up and spiritual maturity are not just a matter of information. They grow from experiences and choices. As a result, the greatest assistance I can provide as a spiritual facilitator is to help people reflect on their own experience. I can aid this by creating space and conditions conducive to reflection and by asking good questions. I can help people be purposeful but I must be careful not to rescue or think I can accelerate the process. Life grows at its own pace. So too do our souls. Most of the work of the spiritual facilitator involves waiting. I might wait years before the time comes that I can help. We must be patient and trust that God is always at work.

THE GREATEST ASSISTANCE I CAN PROVIDE AS A SPIRITUAL FACILITATOR IS TO HELP PEOPLE REFLECT ON THEIR OWN EXPERIENCE.

Maturity

Throughout my life, I sat in religious circles and listened to others say that I needed to give everything to God and become completely dependent on Him. As I reflect on this, I realize that this statement at face value has always made me feel uncomfortable. In part, because I have seen too many people use it as an excuse to take no responsibility for their actions. But more importantly because it flies in the face of what the Scripture paints as the picture of spiritual formation. Paul describes the spiritual growth process as ending in our maturity, not in our dependence.

> *He handed out gifts above and below, filled heaven with his gifts, filled earth with his gifts. He handed out gifts of apostle, prophet, evangelist, and pastor-teacher to train Christians in skilled servant work, working within Christ's body, the church, until we're all moving rhythmically and easily with each other, efficient and graceful in response to God's Son, fully mature adults, fully developed within and without, fully alive like Christ.*

> *No prolonged infancies among us, please. We'll not tolerate babes in the woods, small children who are an easy mark for impostors. God wants us to grow up, to know the whole truth and tell it in love—like Christ in everything. We take our lead from Christ, who is the source of everything we do* (Ephesians 4:11-15).

Thinking about the intent toward which a spiritual facilitator is working, maturity would include the ability to think for oneself, to determine one's own beliefs, to articulate those beliefs, and to serve something larger than one's self-interest. It does not mean that we are our own source of truth; however, the alternative—waiting to be told what to do, what to believe, how to live, and how to view God and others—is a dangerous position to be in. The truth is we too often put ourselves in positions that depend on other people's interpretation of God. In the end, we may be like the apostles in the boat during the storm.* When things got really bad they ran to wake up Jesus. They did not wake him out of confidence but to scold him because they did not trust him to care for them. Their fear challenged all that they had heard. There was still a lack of experience with Jesus' acting on their behalf. In fact, it may not have been until Jesus' reunion with Peter around a fishermen's fire on the beach that it really began to sink in.** This faith he has taught us can be trusted, just like Jesus can be trusted.

There is one other aspect to maturity that we must not forget. To this point we have talked about more of an intellectual maturity. Yet a picture of maturity is not complete until we consider the emotional nature of maturity. If we are to reach out to those most in need, we cannot be controlled by our fear. One of the benefits of thinking for oneself rather than memorizing the "right answers" is that the clearer I become about what I believe, the more open and non-judgmental I can become toward those who are different than me. Too many Christians are reactive, defensive, caustic, and judgmental because they lack emotional maturity. The fact that they have not asked the difficult questions in life for themselves but have depended upon

> Maturity is a product of a growing trust and confidence in God and His actions toward us.

---

*Mark 4:35-44
**John 21

someone else telling them the right answers has left them unprepared to deal with differences. They have been taught to associate only with those who agree with them. Too often such people have a very low tolerance for emotional discomfort. This drives the need for everything to be explained in black-and-white terms. Maturity is a product of a growing trust and confidence in God and His actions toward us. We only come to experience this truth when we risk the important questions.

An Experienced Faith

Jesus begins the great prayer on his final night with the disciples this way: "You put him [Jesus] in charge of everything human so he might give real and eternal life to all in his charge. And this is the real and eternal life: That they **know you**, the one and only true God and Jesus Christ whom you sent" [emphasis added] (John 17:2-3, *The Message*).

I always find it helpful when I am trying to understand the bigger picture to go back to the Scriptures. The sayings and folklore that we grow up with are often taken for grated; however, it is refreshing to set aside my assumptions and see what was actually said.

This is one of the most direct, straightforward statements made by Jesus about the intent of his life. In a very simple way, he connects eternal life with knowing God and the Son. The obvious question is what does "know" mean? For most of the past 100 years or so, knowing has been associated with information, specifically the acquisition of information. In the United States the entire education system has been focused on disseminating information. In the corporate world, billions of dollars are spent every year on documenting, storing, disseminating, and retrieving information. The church was also influenced by this information age. The belief is that if we know more *about* God—if we form all the "right" answers to life's most important questions—then we will know God. Consequently, congregations invest large amounts of time, resources, and energy to the information in the Bible. Even worship has been affected. In many protestant churches, the central point in the service is the sermon, the pastor's attempt to talk about God.

The word "know" in this passage actually means, "a knowledge grounded on personal experience" (Strong, 1977). Knowing someone in this way is much different than knowing about that person. The key here, in my mind, is experience. To achieve this we need a different kind of interaction with others. At some point we cannot simply talk about God, or imagine God, or even talk to God. Experience comes from action. We must take caution, however, at this point. We cannot confuse action with busyness. Doing church activities or even charitable things will not lead us to experience God if the actions we are taking are to get something or to prove something. The action we must take comes from a deep faith in God's view of us. We act out of an identity that is formed by understanding and trusting God's actions on our behalf. Our actions are always a response to God's action for us. We are not the initiator.

We act out of an identity that is formed by understanding and trusting God's actions on our behalf.

Even so, to really experience God we must first start with accepting what truly is. Most of our view of God is a projection of what we want to believe. We want to trust God so we see ourselves trusting God but we live out of a different belief. Let me give you a personal example. I have struggled with the part of prayer that asks God to do things. As I reflected on this one day, a truth became evident. I do not ask God to intervene because I don't believe He will. At some deeper level, there is always a piece of me that does not trust that God cares enough about me to intervene for me. I realized that I have friends that I would ask for help and never doubt that it would be given. I do not have that confidence with God. There is a lack of real experience here. Now there are a number of reasons why I got to this point, many of them of my own device. That is not the point. The point is that if I am to ever really experience God, I have to start by accepting that this is the true state of my relationship with Him. To know and experience someone else, I must be authentic and honest, especially with myself.

To know and experience someone else, I must be authentic and honest, especially with myself.

There is a second necessary component to experienced faith. At some point **we must be willing to take a risk, to become vulnerable to the other.** We cannot always remain in control (or what we believe is in control), maintaining our autonomy and ever really come to experience and trust the other. Why is it that the disciples, in the end, really did come to know Jesus? Part of the reason is that they risked revealing who they really were to Jesus. This included asking hard questions, not concealing their fear, and sharing real experiences that required dependence. For whatever we think about James' and John's seeking of power,* the constant bickering about who among them was the greatest,** their panic-stricken accusations of Jesus' lack of action during a storm,*** these were the events that tested their relationship with Jesus and proved his loyalty.

What we often do not realize is that our lack of intimacy with others, including God, is related to our own need for security. We may fear that there is something unlikable in us so we hide ourselves. An experienced faith grows out of pushing beyond these self-constraints. We must risk acting out of and trusting that we are reconciled to God. This does not happen by learning and memorizing rehearsed answers to all of life's problems. It does not happen by keeping ourselves consumed with attending church functions. No, Jesus seemed to tell us in Matthew 25 that there is a relationship between compassion and our experience of God. But these are not acts of pity exercised from a distance, for that only ends up in the exploitation of another's need for my own self-satisfaction. No, the compassion that leads us to an experienced faith is an action that grows out of a willingness to touch our own need.

THE COMPASSION THAT LEADS US TO AN EXPERIENCED FAITH IS AN ACTION THAT GROWS OUT OF A WILLINGNESS TO TOUCH OUR OWN NEED.

> *Compassion means to become close to the one who suffers. But we can come close to another person only when we are willing to become vulnerable ourselves... The suffering person calls us to become aware of our own suffering. How can I respond to someone's loneliness unless I am in touch with my own experience of loneliness?* (NOUWEN, 1994, P. 105).

Only when I risk accepting the need I have for God to act for me, for others to act for me, will I risk a faith born out of dependence. This is the faith that allows us to truly understand and trust God. This

---

* Mark 10:35-40
** Luke 22:24-30
*** Mark 4: 35-41

is not a faith that expects everyone to live happily ever after in our own design of success. Rather, it is a faith that comes to know that, regardless of my ability to love or respond, God's attitude toward me grows out of who He is, not what I do.

> REGARDLESS OF MY ABILITY TO LOVE OR RESPOND, GOD'S ATTITUDE TOWARD ME GROWS OUT OF WHO HE IS, NOT WHAT I DO.

There was a time in college when I found myself, late one night, standing on a public basketball court cursing God. For the first time in years, I had come to the end of my rope. A long series of rejections and broken dreams had taken their toll. I finally came to the place where I had no other choice but to vent my anger. It was my pursuit of "God's plan" for my life that had continued to be an obstacle in finding my place in the world. Because I had to continue to choose the "plan" over relationships with others, I was alone. It was there, for the first time in my life, that I experienced this truth about God. It was the truth that Abraham learned from God's covenant with him.* It was the truth that Peter experienced on the beach so long ago.** As I felt the embrace of God, I knew that even if I could not believe in Him, He believed in and accepted me. His love for me was not contingent upon me; it was an expression of who He is. For the first time, I had a faith that was experienced. This event was one of several over the next few years that led me to truly understand the breadth and depth of God's commitment to us. It broadened my view of the spiritual and it opened my heart to others. It led me back to compassion, for now I knew what it meant to touch my own suffering only to find that God touched it with me.

Community

Maturity, identity, and experienced faith are all extremely important in the process of spiritual formation. This is true for the individual and for the community as a whole. But more important to this discussion is the fact that they are not characteristics that can be developed in isolation from others. If the individual is to develop maturity, a clear identity, and an experienced faith, he or she will need the help of others. These characteristics can only be developed in community.

---

*Genesis 15
**John 22

Spiritual growth, as it has been defined to this point, is the result of a deep learning at the level of assumptions and emotional response. We cannot become clear about the assumptions we make or the manner in which we react until those things are reflected back to us in our contact with others, and in particular, others who differ from us. The church has done a poor job of creating containers or an environment where people of different perspectives come to know and learn together. On the contrary, many churches have an unspoken agenda, aiming to get everyone believing the same things and living the same way. So those who are outside the defined norm of that specific congregation are, at best, marginalized within the church or, at worst, driven out as threats or troublemakers. The result is that the congregation works against the maturing of the members.

WE CANNOT BECOME CLEAR ABOUT THE ASSUMPTIONS WE MAKE OR THE MANNER IN WHICH WE REACT UNTIL THOSE THINGS ARE REFLECTED BACK TO US IN OUR CONTACT WITH OTHERS, AND IN PARTICULAR, OTHERS WHO DIFFER FROM US.

The church community, above all places, should be a place of safety where people come and find acceptance of who they are regardless of where they may be in life. It should be the place where people who doubt their value come to be reminded that they are of great worth. The actions of God on our behalf communicate His belief in our worth. The church should be a place where people come to learn to be less afraid of other people. We need a place where we can become less fragmented—from ourselves, others, God, and our world—not a place where we hide behind the "Christian" persona, fearful that others will see us for who we really are.

The result of this type of community is really two-fold. First, members learn the critical abilities needed to develop their spiritual identity. The abilities to listen, wait, be honest with self and others, confess, and grow our faith are developed as much by how we talk to and treat others as in what we talk about. This is a critical point often missed in our church communities. Over time, God perfects His work in us as He helps us grow up (Ephesians 4). The second result is a community of people who treat each other dramatically differently than any other place in the world. This "love for one another" is what Jesus told us in John 17 would make the difference in the world, as people would wonder if his message was true.

What are the Implications for the Spiritual Facilitator?

First, focusing on an individualized faith misses much of the point. Christianity does have individual choice and responsibility as a part of it. Yet it is the communal nature of the church that prepares the individual for growth and acts as the greatest testimony to the truth of Christ.

Second, the facilitator must be as focused on how members interact as on what they interact about. It is not enough to communicate truth if that truth is communicated in a way that hinders the members from growing up or experiencing their faith. To borrow a phrase from the corporate training fields, "Telling ain't training." Stating a belief is not living that faith. Talking about God is not enough, especially if we use talking about God to avoid encountering God.

A third implication is that the spiritual facilitator cannot be too quick to rescue others from their difficulties. Suffering, which is a normal part of life, is also a critical component in spiritual development.

Finally, the spiritual facilitator must pay close attention to his or her own sense of self. Identity, to be real, is owned and comes from within. To promote maturity in others, one must also be mature. To remain connected to others even when it is difficult, requires one to be mature emotionally and capable of withstanding the discomfort of difference, conflict, or chaos.

2 The Context of Adventure

The shaping elements of spiritual formation are community, risk, trust, and acceptance. We struggle and in that struggle we learn to ask different and more important questions. Spiritual formation has as its end a faith that comes from the trial and error of experience. If we want to accelerate the maturity of an experienced faith, how and where do we do it? We must recognize that this is not a kind of learning and development that we truly control. We cannot plan for breakthrough moments. Profound change cannot be predicted, yet we can create containers that may improve the possibility that we might see what God is doing. An ideal container for finding the crossroad moments of life is adventure. In the next few chapters, we will look at what adventure is, why it works to help us learn the profound lessons in life, and how we can create intentional encounters with the unknown through purposeful experience.

THE SHAPING ELEMENTS OF SPIRITUAL FORMATION ARE COMMUNITY, RISK, TRUST, AND ACCEPTANCE.

What Is Adventure?

Adventure is an experience where the outcome is unknown. It is a definition that can be applied to a wide range of things. In this book, adventure refers to a range of experiences that include active adventures like backpacking, rock climbing, rafting, caving, challenge courses, cross-cultural service projects, and pilgrimages as well as less-active adventures such as retreat, counseling, and solitude. Adventure is not limited to these activities but they are especially good containers for the kind of learning this book explores.

Why Adventure?

Dragging himself up from the river's bottom, wet clothes clinging to him as if to impede any progress, Jesus emerged from his baptism. What is the first thing he did after experiencing the public revelation of who he was and what the Father thought of him?

> *Then Jesus was led out into the wilderness by the Holy Spirit to be tempted there by the Devil* (MATTHEW 4:1).

Jesus' public life began with an extended adventure trip. He was led into the wilderness where he spent 40 days wrestling with who he was and what voice he would trust for the remainder of his life. I wonder why that was? What is it about the wilderness, adventure, solitude, and reflection that make it the ideal container for spiritual formation?

New and Unfamiliar Environment

The challenge for most of us is to find enough space to begin to sort out the voices that we actually listen to. Our normal lives and homes are filled with props, shortcuts, distractions, and duties—business that keeps us from having to ask the difficult questions. Our roles, responsibilities, friends, and family provide unsuspected cover, enabling us to continue pursuing our own agendas and seeking our own sources of certainty. If we are to discover who we really are, we must have a change of context. Adventure provides a rich environment for learning to see with new eyes.

ADVENTURE PROVIDES A RICH ENVIRONMENT FOR LEARNING TO SEE WITH NEW EYES.

To begin with, whether we are on a pilgrimage, a challenge course, a mission trip, or wilderness retreat, the world of adventure pursuits is always a much simpler place. There are few modern conveniences. We are often limited by what we can carry. The agenda in the world of adventure is much more basic. Getting from one place to the next,

WE ARE OFTEN LIMITED BY WHAT WE CAN CARRY.

eating, drinking, sleeping, and shelter are about all the concerns a day without modern conveniences will allow. The problems presented in this context are generally clear and straightforward. There are not many political implications. Build a shelter or get wet. Start a fire or be cold. Make the climb or walk away. It is in the midst of these simpler but no less important struggles that we find we have space to consider who we are, why we are, and where we are going from here.

For most, there is also novelty in the environment. There are few experts around to solve things for us. The natural environment has a humbling way of making us all equal and at times quite small. Without the certainties and confidence that our knowledge, power, expertise, and training provide us, we have no choice but to begin to look for answers wherever we might find them. The most unassuming member of a group often sees the path forward most clearly, but for this direction to be helpful, all members must be willing to submit to insight regardless of who offers it. If we are overly bigoted about whose help we are willing to take, we will struggle mightily in the context of adventure where the natural world offers no respect to status. The same is true for our spirits.

> *Virtually everything in the North American way of life has led us to think we are in charge of our lives, that we are the measure of all things, that everything depends on us. We are traveling a broad road paved with good intentions, expertly engineered with the latest technologies to get us to where someone has told us we want to go, and we want to get there with the least inconvenience, efficiently and quickly. It is a heavily trafficked road, noisy and polluted, with many accidents and fatalities* (Peterson, 2005, p. 308).

How can we look to a source other than our own productivity for a clue to our identities until we see this illusion for what it is? So immersing ourselves in a world where we cannot control (or even maintain the illusion of control) is a first step to "repentance," "a change in direction" (Peterson, 2005, p. 308).

Perhaps what changes most in the adventure environment is the pace and the quietness of life. Without the technological distractions of cell phones, Internet, television, planes, trains, or automobiles, life quickly becomes very local and very particular. In the wilderness, we don't really care what the weather is 10, or even 5, miles away. We care about the weather at our location. The world without technology shrinks to the small area where we live and are right now. The pace of this much smaller world slows us down and allows us to see what we cannot see at a much faster pace. We are introduced to a new rhythm of life that is set by the rising and setting of the sun. We cannot turn on stimulation and put our minds to sleep. We have time to think, consider, ponder, and most importantly listen. As we develop our attentiveness to that which is most local and particular to our location, we begin to hear new voices. It may start with the true voices of our fears, worries, or complaints. Within these troubles are the hidden notes of our current assumptions and the first measures of the truth we must face if we are to find our true identities.

We cannot turn on stimulation and put our minds to sleep.

An Element of Risk

When the outcome of the task is uncertain and our skills untried, the adventure takes place. "Confronted with the real possibility of success and failure, the learning experience often takes an element of excitement or what has been referred to as optimal arousal" (Ewert, 1989). When we truly face the mystery of what we cannot foreknow or control, we become dependent. Not dependent in terms of not being to take action on our own, but dependent in the sense that we will not have those things that typically provide us with security. We will experience real uncertainty about what we think we know. More important than the physical risk we face in the pursuit of adventure is that we come face to face with the real potential of failure. It is an emotional shift that opens up the path to enlightenment. Mystery is at the heart of who we are and the relationship that we have with God. It is when we are willing to come in contact with what we do not know and cannot control that we meet new questions and more importantly new answers that often lead to the next stage of our journey. The physical risk is a sacrament* for what is going on inside us and among us as we seek faith.

---

*Sacrament. a visible sign of an inward grace. Retrieved March 28, 2009, from http://dictionary.reference.com/browse/sacrament.

Immediate and Concrete Consequences

We live in illusory worlds where we are rarely at fault. Our frustrations are forced on us by the actions of others. Our intentions are always pure and right and our mistakes are always a failure of others to understand our intentions. Our minds have a peculiar ability to always remember history significantly slanted in our direction. If we are to develop a faith that is experienced and an identity that is true, we must move beyond this adolescent certainty. In the world of adventure, the consequences of our actions and decisions are immediate, real, and concrete. We may, for awhile, nurse along the illusions of always being right but eventually we will have to come face to face with our choices and their aftermath. The search for spiritual formation calls us to recognize that no matter what others are doing to us or around us, it is our own perspective and responses that are either aligned with our true selves or not. No one can force me to doubt my value, question my acceptance, or limit my willingness to trust. Those are always choices that I make, and the sooner I begin to recognize that, the quicker I can begin to focus on the place where I have some hope of change—within myself.

The Priority of Reflection

"What is of greatest consequence in a person's life is not just the nature and extent of his or her experiences, but what has been learned from them" (Cousins, 1981). With its emphasis on processing, experiential education impresses on participants the importance of thinking and talking about their lives and not blindly moving from one event to another. In a world that moves at full throttle, building commitment to reflection, listening, prayer, and meditation is a real challenge. When we use structured experience to teach, reflection comes naturally as we attempt to overcome new challenges. Over time we learn to ask questions as a way of responding to experiences rather than making assumptions or simply reacting.

Over time we learn to ask questions as a way of responding to experiences rather than making assumptions or simply reacting.

For the spiritual facilitator, the "processing" time that follows important experiences is also the time when we teach others to ask different and often more important questions. For a long time I struggled to get youth to deal with more important questions. They wanted to know what the next activity was, when we would eat, and other such adolescent things. I wanted them to think about their purpose, identity, and faith. A good friend of mine gave me some advice that has changed my way of working with all people. He said, "Don't worry about getting them to ask important questions, you ask them while among them and soon they will ask them for themselves." Reflection is not a practice that can be forced; it can only be chosen. Yet, in the world of adventure and experiential learning, this most basic practice of spiritual formation can be discovered.

The Focus on Support

The adventure education experience builds on success and at the same time defines failure as an opportunity to try again more intelligently. Even the physical support of spotting and belay systems communicates the idea that failure is okay in this group where all who try are supported. We will never develop a mature spirit if we do not risk and more importantly tell the truth about our limitations and failures. In fact, what gets in our way most frequently is the unspoken belief that if we just work hard enough we will not need forgiveness because we can get beyond our own frailty. Adventure always brings us to one of the most important gifts of spiritual formation—failure. At some point, we will be afraid, we will lack concentration, strength, or agility, and we will not know the answer. In that moment, we are poised to learn a great lesson—we all need help. We will learn that spiritual formation is God's work, not ours. We can participate. We can certainly hinder it, but only when we are willing to reach out for help will we be open enough to receive.

> ONLY WHEN WE ARE WILLING TO REACH OUT FOR HELP WILL WE BE OPEN ENOUGH TO RECEIVE.

The physical and emotional support of group members in adventure activities is a sacrament for the life in God. Belayers who are holding the end of the rope catch a climber no matter what. That is their commitment. It does not matter that the climber was afraid, made a mistake, was overconfident, or just flat quit. The belayer catches the climber. This is also a picture of the way it is with God. His chosen response to us is forgiveness. I have found that these lived moments of unconditional support may be the first time a person actually understands that we have been given this gift from God.

The Opportunity for Meaningful Contributions

Every person in an adventure experience has a role to play and an opportunity to contribute to the success of the group. In fact, it is imperative that each participant make his or her contribution if the group is to succeed. This ability to influence a peer group will resound in the heart of someone who may feel insignificant and unimportant in other life situations.

The real lesson for many may come from seeing the contributions of others and the real need that we each have for help. If I try to go it alone or control the group for my own security, all fail to some degree. The best-case scenario is when everyone sees their opportunity for participation and takes action. In these experiences, we come to understand place, context, and gratitude. At least these lessons can be learned if we can get beyond ourselves. We must come to appreciate others for who they are and the value of their presence. In doing so, we begin to learn the humility that is necessary in spiritual formation. When we can step back and make a contribution, not as a hero, but as one of many trying to do the best we can together, we begin to recognize our place in the work of spiritual formation. We may begin to understand what Eugene Peterson says:

> *How do we participate appropriately in this holy community.... As we cultivate fear-of-the-Lord, we develop a reverent respect for what is going on, and then modestly but also in genuine delight begin doing what is there to be done. Practicing fear-of-the-Lord gradually but surely shifts our attention from a preoccupation with what we can or should do to an attentive absorption in what God has been doing...* (Peterson, 2005, p. 301).

Implications for Spiritual Facilitators: To this point, I have been talking about participants and their experience. Before I move on, I do have one idea for the spiritual facilitator. Adventure as a place for meaningful contribution also calls the facilitator to rethink his or her view of others. In adventure, the watching facilitator will frequently be surprised by the source of help and what that help truly is. Adventure makes us lay aside our assumptions about people and simply stay awake for how people will appear. In this environment we can move beyond a trap that often entangles us.

Those whom we consider lazy, indifferent, hostile, or obnoxious we treat as such, forcing them in this way to live up to our own views. And so, much of our ministry is limited by the snares of our own judgments. These self-created limits prevent us from being available to people and shrivel up our compassion (Nouwen, 1981, p. 35).

Conclusion

I have come to believe that we need some very important capabilities (self-awareness, critical reflection, solitude, listening, taking risks) if we are to have healthy spirits. Unfortunately, there are so few places to really learn this type of living. Adventure is one school where we are required to learn this slowed-down, deep-awareness kind of living. If we do not, we will be uncomfortable at best and perhaps injured at worst. How we teach the spiritual life is as important as what we teach. Many may be teaching the right things in the wrong way. The result is a faith that has the right content but no experience.

How we teach the spiritual life is as important as what we teach.

3 What are the Greatest Hurdles to Spiritual Formation?

The most obvious place to begin is sin. Yet our understanding of sin determines whether we will live life with God or settle for the limited security of religion. Sin is more than bad deeds. It is not that our actions are not important, but that this definition of sin does not go far enough. Sin is at the center of what we do, but the corrupting power of sin lies in how it shadows us from understanding our true standing with God. Sin steals from us what God has freely given us—choice, freedom, love, and hope.

Morality is not the opposite of sin. Trust is. Let me explain. Much of the time, we think the battle lies in getting ourselves to stop doing bad things. What makes them bad? The universal quality of sin is that it is an illusion that promises what it can never deliver. It gains strength by drawing on our fear, our doubt, and our mistrust. All of the wrong or unhealthy things I do can be traced back to the fact that I am trying to get something that I think I need, or I am trying to cover up for a perceived lack of what I think I need. I choose to pursue affluence because I believe it will validate my importance. If I am important then I am secure. I lash out at those closest to me because I doubt my standing with them. I may try to prove my worth, but ultimately, this will fail because no one is capable of unconditional acceptance. We all suffer the same self-doubt at some point. We want to be accepted but fear that we are not. So we try to make the world around us into the way believe it should be. Again this validates my worth or at least makes me feel secure. We cannot conquer sin by doing and proving our worth. We can only overcome

Morality is not the opposite of sin.

sin by seeing it for what it is. When we accept and receive we begin to undo the ties of sin that skew our view of ourselves, God, and others. When I stop and receive, I begin to trust that what I need has or will be given to me. I begin to trust that there is more going on in the world than what I can make happen. I stop taking from others what they cannot or will not give. I begin to know God because I stop forcing Him to be what I imagine and I start seeing Him for who He is. I experience love, because love cannot be forced; it can only be given freely and received openly. At the heart of this is trust. I take God at His word and believe that I am accepted. This opens me to loving others. So our real battle is not with keeping moral rules but with understanding and challenging those things that keep us requiring from others what can only be received for free from God. This leads us to deal with our fear, our mistrust, and our ambition.

> I BEGIN TO TRUST THAT THERE IS MORE GOING ON IN THE WORLD THAN WHAT I CAN MAKE HAPPEN.

In the Dark of the Night of Fear

Most of us spend the entirety of our lives learning to avoid contact with those things that frighten us. We keep people at arm's length. We surround ourselves with only those who think like we think, who will behave predictably. It is only in the quiet, often in the dark of the night, that we are startled by those things from which we run. Void of distractions that keep us preoccupied, we remember that there is an unsettledness deep within us. In the midst of the internal chaos lie our worries. I hesitate to use the word "worries," because it seems too trite. What we deeply fear is not trivial. It is deeply important and it is the reason God left heaven to live as one of us.

Fear may be the greatest barrier to our search for faith. John dedicated a significant portion of his first letter to the topic. He tells us "there is no fear in love, for perfect love casts out fear because fear has torment" (I John 4:18). One writer suggests, "Moving beyond fear may be the single most important thing that you can do for yourself. And your planet" (Abdullah, 1999).

Whether we can change the world by becoming less afraid, I am not sure, but I do know this: **If we find ourselves acting as the facilitator of another person's spiritual growth, we will have to deal with fear.** We will have to be acutely aware of our own. We will also have to patiently wait as those we help gather the courage to uncover their own. It is often the presence of another, who does not panic in the face of struggle, who enables us to ask the questions we dare not usually ask. These are the important questions that the spiritual facilitator waits to bring forth.

We all deal with our fears differently. We use a variety of strategies for maintaining our sense of security. We run. We are angry. We medicate. We also practice religion. Yet, if we are to grow our spirits we cannot continue to mask the fear. We must first accept it, acknowledge it, and name it. For me personally, all my great fears are symptomatic of the fear that lies deepest within me, the fear of not being good enough. I suspect that this is true with the most of us. If we are honest, most of what we do, collect, accomplish, and possess is in response to the question, "What makes me valuable?" We act in self-destructive ways to cover up the truth that we may not be good enough. We also spend a great deal of time perfecting our goodness for the same reason.

If we are to grow our spirits we cannot continue to mask the fear.

The first and most important idea that we need to see and help others see is that we are valuable; we are okay because God said so. Jesus' life and death tell us this is so. The manner of his death is meant to tell us that there is nothing we can do that will change the value God places on us. This is paramount. This is the most important message of all the ages. We are loved and accepted by God. He has reconciled us to Himself (Colossians 1). The real mystery of this truth is that it is so, not because of what we do or can do, but because that is who God is. We can spend our lives chasing our tails trying to prove that we are good enough. However, it is only when we stop trying to prove ourselves that we can see what has been before us all the time. God loves us and we can love ourselves, too.

> *My dear children, let's not just talk about love; let's practice real love. This is the only way we'll know we're living truly, living in God's reality. It's also the way to shut down the debilitating self-criticism, even when there is something to it. For God is greater than our worried hearts and knows more about us than we do ourselves. And friends, once that's taken care of and we're no longer accusing or condemning ourselves, we're bold and free before God* (I John 3:18-21, The Message).

Spiritual facilitators cannot come at this fear directly. Not at first anyway. People are much too adept at hiding from their shadows. I have found that we must only bite off what we can chew at the moment. What keeps me trying to get to the bottom of it is someone who reminds me of who I am, continuing to trust the process even if I do not. That is the role of the spiritual friend, facilitator, and guide.

Our work is quiet work. We listen and talk. We act and reflect. But what we do most is help others trust their acceptance when they cannot trust it for themselves. We are the voice that tells them what no other voice is saying. You matter. You are important. And most importantly, I can think this because God thinks it first. I have a good friend that has been instrumental in being that voice in my life. In fact, we echo this truth to each other, for what we see so clearly about the other is often experienced with great distance and darkness for ourselves. I once attended a midday communion service with him at a large downtown church. There were all of six in attendance and three of them worked for the church. When we left, I asked him why a church would continue to do that service with so few in attendance. His response was that the priest would do it if no one else was there. He does so because he is remembering for those who cannot remember for themselves. That is the work of the disciple maker. We may give many talks, teach many lessons, attend many activities with those we serve, but the most important work is helping them to hear for themselves that they are loved and accepted.

The second piece of work we can do is stay connected to people. There will come a time in their growth that they will lose faith in the process of searching and listening for God. It is at this moment that we can lend them some courage and will until they can supply their own. We can support them and urge them to continue when they come into contact with those questions that scare them the most, when their lives are in turmoil. Spiritual facilitators can help by asking the questions that will lead seekers out of uncertainty and maintaining the conditions that make this questioning possible. It is not our job to tell people who to be or to make them into the image we feel most appropriate. It is our job to provide a space for people to ask the questions that no one else will help them ask. It is our job to reflect back to them what is given to us—the love of God.

It is our job to provide a space for people to ask the questions that no one else will help them ask.

I was working with a group of women on a ropes course recently. Although these were leaders in daily life, they were struggling with working and leading together. From my perspective, each person was so focused on providing the answer to the challenge that no one was really listening to the others. My question to them was, "What do you believe leadership is? I asked that question because I believe it was their definition or paradigm of leadership that had them trapped in repeating the same mistake over and over. This was a question that sought to move beyond the obvious and open the space into the deeper-held assumptions that formed their actions. The spiritual facilitator is called to do the same. We must look beyond behavior and ask questions that get to the underlying beliefs.

Mistrust

An important realization that I came to several years ago is that this fear that limits our experience with God's grace comes from a deeper mistrust. If we were really honest with ourselves we would admit that a part of us does not trust God. We hope, we want to believe, but in the end we really do not trust that the story of our acceptance is really true. This is a significant reason behind why we are so tied to morality as the way to fix our world. If we are good, then all things being fair, life will turn out well for us.

> SOME PORTION OF ADAM AND EVE DID NOT FULLY TRUST GOD EVEN THOUGH HE WALKED WITH THEM REGULARLY.

This barrier of mistrust goes all the way back to the beginning. Adam and Eve made the choices they made not to be rebellious or in a fit of arrogance. The serpent exploited a critical characteristic in them. Some portion of Adam and Eve did not fully trust God even though He walked with them regularly. They did not trust that they had all that was necessary for life and happiness. They put faith in the illusion that there was more—that God was holding back.

We are no different. We seek security in our possessions, our titles, our status, our morality because we do not really trust that God's pronouncement of our wholeness is enough. If we do not work to reveal this barrier, we will continue to chase that illusion. We will spend a lifetime trying to get from others what only God has provided for free—unconditional acceptance. It is real and we can experience it if we dare to trust it.

4 Understanding the Dynamics of Change

Discipleship is the lifetime process of spiritual formation. What does this mean? Although spiritual formation may have many different meanings, for me it has come to represent the core work of faith development—learning to trust who God says we are. The centerpiece of the mystery, as Paul calls it, is that we are no longer enemies with God. We have been reconciled and are seen as perfect and holy in God's eyes (I Corinthians 1). This may be true, but we have a very difficult time trusting this reality. We struggle to hope it is true, but living out of this truth is a very different thing. Discipleship is an intentional journey toward letting who God says I am define who I am. If I can come to trust this identity, then I will see others, myself, and my purpose in life much differently.

So the critical question for this chapter is, "How do we change or learn to reshape our identity?" The learning that occurs at this level is much more than the acquisition of new information. The learning we are discussing requires us to shift our fundamental assumptions about who we are, our image of God, and how we believe the world works. But this intellectual change is preceded by an emotional shift. We cannot learn at this level if we are driven by the need for comfort, security, certainty, and control. We must increase our ability to tolerate emotional discomfort and the sense of being lost that comes with challenging our identity and worldview. We must come to trust that we can risk asking questions that will lead us to new understanding and not lose our faith in the process. We must trust that as long as we are seeking the truth, the Holy Spirit will help guide us to the truth even if we cannot see the path.* This is an endeavor that requires great courage, yet we can remove some of the mystery if we understand the dynamics of this type of learning.

The Dynamics of Spiritual Formation

Defining Learning

We will begin with the end in mind and start by further defining learning. Two of the dominant forces in the New Testament approach the question of spiritual formation from very different perspectives, yet our definition of learning will be able to accommodate both. Paul tends to focus on the intellectual shifts that occur as God's unconditional acceptance increasingly becomes the defining source for us. His most famous passage is in Romans 12:2, "Don't copy the behavior and customs of the world, but let God transform you into a new person by changing the way you think..." The Greek work *metanoeo*, which translates to *repent* in English, means to "think differently" (Strong, 1977). If we are to let the Gospel message form us, we must change the way we think. We must surface and challenge our deepest assumptions. Our assumptions form the internal logic that drives our behavior. Much of our poor behavior is the result of a flawed internal logic built on deep-seated assumptions. Paul saw that we must understand how God sees us if we are to shift our thinking. If I think that God only accepts me if I am perfect, then I will focus on things like keeping the rules. In my experience, this focus brings much angst, fear, self-doubt, and even a good dose of righteous indignation. But if, as Paul reminds us, I see myself as "holy and blameless... without a single fault" (I Corinthians 1:22), then I will focus on very different things. I will not have to work on getting God's approval but on accepting God's approval, which I already have. My focus becomes uncovering my lack of trust, which leads me to take action to earn or prove the acceptance that I already have for free.

> LEARNING IS THE PROCESS BY WHICH WE CHALLENGE OUR ASSUMPTIONS IN ORDER TO RECOVER WHO GOD SAYS WE ARE.

---

*The most profound truths of who we are, are paradoxical in nature. Mark 9:35, Luke 9:24

The apostle John, on the other hand, seemed to speak to an emotional shift. In the fourth chapter of his first letter, he spends a good amount of time talking about driving out fear. In John's mind, fear and love were incompatible. In fact, driving out self-doubt and fear opens us to receiving what God is giving us. This is subtle but very important. Spiritual formation—spiritual maturity—is a work of God, not our work. We play a role, but our work is primarily a responsive one. We receive, accept, and trust. God forms, develops, and grows us. But we cannot participate well when we are anxious, reactive, and fearful. Changing our minds requires us to consider new things that will at the same time contradict some of the old ways of thinking. As we let go of what we thought we knew to take hold of new thoughts, there is a time when we are uncertain. If we run from that discomfort we will never see the new perspective. We will settle for old answers that we know even if those answers do not work. So part of the learning we do is to slow down so we will be more purposeful and less reactive. How do we respond to those who are different from us? If our first response to an idea different from ours is "No, that cannot be true," then we will not learn. But if we can listen first and discern after we understand the different perspective, then we have a very good chance of learning.

> LEARNING INVOLVES AN EMOTIONAL SHIFT THAT COMES AS WE RISK THE DISCOMFORT OF THE UNKNOWN.

So learning involves a change of mind, which happens as we become aware of the assumptions that we hold. It also involves an emotional shift that comes as we risk the discomfort of the unknown. When we do not panic but tolerate the emotional discomfort, we remain open, which is necessary to change.

Learning Begins With Disturbance

Learning is not the beginning but the end. So how do we get to the learning? **It is important to realize that all learning begins with a disturbance.** A disturbance can be something internal to us or external to us that tells us it is time to be different. Thoughtful teachings, coming into contact with a different culture, a fight with a friend—these are all examples of disturbances. I would also

> A DISTURBANCE CAN BE SOMETHING INTERNAL OR EXTERNAL TO US THAT TELLS US IT IS TIME TO BE DIFFERENT.

suggest that sin is a disturbance. When I do something wrong, or when I hurt someone else, or I act in a way that is inconsistent with who I really am, I will experience consequences. Those consequences can be internal in the form of conviction, guilt, or regret. They can also be external, resulting in destructive behavior and/or broken relationships. All of these things tell us that our worldview is skewed and we need to adjust if we are to return to the peace of living whole. Sometimes disturbances come in the form of questions. When I wake up and see that my formula for living is not really working, and I begin to ask questions that challenge my status quo, I experience disturbance. In the ancient world, prophets were a predominant form of disturbance. A prophet had two jobs—tell the honest truth about what was, and stretch people's thinking by describing what could be. Both of those messages act as disturbance. They call us to be different.

> At the point of disturbance, we can chose to move toward or away from our spiritual maturity.

At the point of disturbance, we can chose to move toward or away from our spiritual maturity. Just because we experience a disturbance does not mean that we will heed it. We often ignore our disturbances or rationalize them away. Allowing ourselves to be disturbed is like opening Pandora's Box. It is like Neo in *The Matrix*, who takes the pill and wakes up. We cannot predict where the disturbance will take us. Yet we cannot learn or grow if we do not take the risk.

If we do take the risk, there is a very good probability that we will experience some chaos. Chaos, the period of uncertainty between when we let go of what we know but have not fully grasped what might be, can be a powerful and misunderstood part of the transformation process. Chaos, though called different things, has long been a part of our heritage. At its most intense, it is the "dark night of the soul" where our old identities are wrestled away from us. It can also be experienced as anxiety, fear, guilt, or doubt. We often think that the chaos is the enemy that we must overcome immediately, when in reality, chaos can be the unusual companion that ushers us to a clearer grasp of the mystery. Because we fear it, we often take actions that give us relief in the short run, but do not really move us toward learning. In fact, when we find solace

> Chaos is the period of uncertainty between when we let go of what we know but have not fully grasped what might be.

in these quick-fix responses, we make it that much more difficult for real change to occur. This is so because first, each time we take the comfort of the quick fix, we reduce our capacity to tolerate the discomfort that is necessary to truly change. It is also true, because we make it harder for the next disturbance to awaken us.

Responding to Chaos

What are some of these quick-fix responses? On the surface few of these actions appear to be more than they are, yet if we understand the underlying cause they serve, we can see them as quite injurious to our spirits. The first quick fix I want to suggest is **confession**. Now, this might seem like a contradiction since confession is clearly a critical part of spiritual formation. Yet there is a form of confession that does not free us but rather reinforces a vision of God that continues to trap us. For me, this type of confession always involved a high degree of panicked guilt and some very intense **deal-making**. When we are in chaos, we want affirmation that everything is alright, that there is order in the world. So, we often turn to making deals with God in order to avoid punishment.

In chaos, we often turn to making deals with God in order to avoid punishment.

I remember when my daughter was quite young, just three or four, she had been having one of those days. She had been pushing every limit and every button that I had. I was tired, and she pushed me that last inch. I reminded her of the authority I had as her parent. Just as I was about to execute her sentence, she looked at me and asked, "Are you sure there's not something I could do about this?" Needless to say, after I pulled myself back together and stopped laughing, she received a reprieve and our day ended quite nicely. We are not so different with God. We push our behavior beyond the limits and then believe that if we make the right deal, He won't be mad and punish us. We may get a sense of relief out of this exchange, but we keep ourselves trapped in the belief that, first of all, God's tendency is to punish us. It also keeps us from looking deeper at our experience to discover how we came to be there in the first place. Sin is often an impetuous act to get something we think we need. If we only see it as a desperate act that we must make amends for, we lose the opportunity to challenge the underlying assumptions that keep us stuck in that cycle of behavior. Deal-making is a quick response designed for one thing—our comfort. It will not bring us to a better understanding of ourselves or God.

Another quick-fix response is **blame**. In the church it is quite accepted to view the "world" or Satan as the reason we are feeling as we do. The reality is that most of what we would call sin is the result of our own lack of awareness, integrity, and trust. When we make our actions the result of an enemy out there, we do feel better for the moment, but again we lose the opportunity to really see inside ourselves. We become very indignant and motivated to defeat the enemy while remaining blind to the fact that the real enemy stares back at us in the mirror every morning. It may seem noble to ride out to defeat a great foe, but it keeps us distracted from the real work of spiritual formation. God calls us to consider the expanse of His gift and challenge the underlying mistrust we have in that gift. When we focus on external reasons for why we do not hold tight to our acceptance, we run the risk of always believing something else must change before we can experience the gift of God. The only thing that must change is our fear and determination to prove our worth.

When we make our actions the result of an enemy out there, we do feel better for the moment, but we lose the opportunity to really see inside ourselves.

A third response to chaos is to attempt to **take control**. The thing about chaos that troubles us most is the uncertainty of it all. So in an attempt to regain a sense of security, we try to take control. There is a broad range of actions that fall under this heading, but there are two that I want to bring to the forefront. First, taking control naturally places our focus on other people and/or circumstances. As we try to take control, we often attempt to get others to do or be what we want, or we try to manipulate circumstances to make them who we need them to be. The real problem here is that we have no power to do either, so we grow frustrated and anxious because others will not cooperate and/or our circumstances cannot be manipulated. The more anxious we become, the greater our chaos, so the harder we try to take and keep control.

Taking control naturally places our focus on other people and/or circumstances.

A second and more subtle way of taking control is to remove the mystery. It is the unknown of chaos that is so troubling and so we remove the mystery or the unknown by defining, prescribing, or eliminating. Faith is hard to understand because it is a very mysterious concept, so we attempt to make it concrete. We define what it is and what it is not. This allows us to establish criteria that enable us to quickly determine if something or someone is faithful. The problem with this practice is that faith requires that we embrace mystery. We take control by creating definitions, rules, policies, and criteria that allow us to bring stability to uncomfortable situations. If we can name something, then we feel as if we know it; and if we know it, we can control it to some degree. We eliminate our chaos, but we limit any ability to learn or to see things from a new perspective.

> A more subtle way of taking control is to remove the mystery.

A fourth way we deal with the tension of chaos is **busyness**. Doing something almost always feels better than doing nothing. When we are uncertain, we start taking action. The darkness of chaos is calling us to a new understanding but to see the new understanding we must be able to tolerate the loneliness of waiting. For example, we feel uncomfortable by the suffering of others, so we want to fix it. There is nothing wrong with doing things, but when our busyness is a way to avoid what we fear, then it is not serving us well. What we might need more is to touch that suffering in order to experience the grace that suffering brings. Busyness can lead us to hyperactivity that can lead to burn out or to rescuing others in order to relieve our own discomfort with the potential failure of another. It limits our ability to grow spiritually. "You know that this is the compulsiveness that keeps us going and busy but at the same time makes us wonder whether we are getting anywhere in the long run. This is the way to spiritual exhaustion and burnout. This is the way to spiritual death" (Nouwen, 2006, p. 32).

> Doing something almost always feels better than doing nothing.

Moving From Chaos to Learning

How then do we proceed from chaos to learning? Like most of life's important transitions, the path is paradoxical. When we are experiencing chaos, our natural response is to take hold and grip tighter in an effort to regain our control. We grasp at what we know or think we know, and in so doing, we close ourselves off from ideas, perceptions, and truths that may be difficult and challenging but are also the path to maturity. **The response that will move us from chaos to learning is to let go.** This is not giving away our senses or responsibilities. It is loosening our grip on things that would keep us closed to new possibilities. We may need to loosen our grip on many things, such as our ego, past experience, preconceived ideas, and our prejudices. But there are three that I want to elaborate on because of their impact on spiritual formation.

> LETTING GO IS LOOSENING OUR GRIP ON THINGS THAT WOULD KEEP US CLOSED TO NEW POSSIBILITIES.

The first area we must loosen our grip on is our need for **control**. As we discussed in the last section, we seek to take control, particularly of others and circumstances when we are threatened. What we need to do is see that for what it is—an illusion. We control neither others nor circumstances, but we can control ourselves. How we choose to respond to new ideas or people who are different from us will determine how much we grow. Many churches and organizations have a great need to fix, heal, or convert people who are different from "the norm" of that particular community. If we are to learn, we must let go of that need and choose to be vulnerable. Our vulnerability brings with it a measure of humility that allows us to fully hear the ideas, perceptions, and/or experiences of others before we respond. There is a risk in being vulnerable, for we may appear as weak or unsophisticated. That is a risk we must be willing to take. Ultimately, this need for control betrays what is really at the heart of our spiritual struggles—mistrust. As Henri Nouwen warns us, we turn to power rather than trust or love. "What makes the temptation of power so seemingly irresistible? Maybe it is that power offers an easy substitute for the hard task of love. It seems easier to be God than to love God, easier to control people than to love people, easier to own life than to love life" (1989, p. 590). Opening ourselves to the real influence of others or God is an intentional act of trust, and it is a necessity if we want to grow into our true identity.

The second thing we must let go of is our need for **certainty**. By this I mean the need to be right. The confidence of the evangelical movement comes from their unflinching belief that they hold the right answers. There is nothing wrong with having a sense of truth, nor is there anything wrong with having beliefs and answers that help us explain the world. The problem comes when being right is the most important thing. When we need to be right we only listen to see if the words of the other are in agreement with our own. We do not listen for any truth that we might not know, we listen to confirm or deny what is being said by the other. We then take appropriate actions by completely agreeing with things we also hold true or defending our positions to those who disagree with us. We may also just walk away or discount others if their positions are too far astray of our own. The point is we quit listening when we have a need to be right. We settle for pleasantries or debate but we close ourselves off from any new influence in our lives. We must have a bit of uncertainty to make us curious. It is that curiosity that will keep leading us back to the Truth. Each time we pass God, we will know a bit more; we must be open to the new things that God has to teach us.

WHEN WE NEED TO BE RIGHT WE ONLY LISTEN TO SEE IF THE WORDS OF THE OTHER ARE IN AGREEMENT WITH OUR OWN.

A third area we must consider when letting go is our need for **comfort**. So much of spiritual formation requires us to take risks. Yet we too often seek to maintain our comfort. Our spirits grow when we risk faith, compassion, love, and acceptance. If we are to approach any of these, we must be willing to tolerate some discomfort. Take compassion, which is a type of openness that allows the suffering of others to influence us. "Compassion means to become close to the one who suffers. But we can come close to another person only when we are willing to become vulnerable ourselves" (Nouwen, 1994, p. 105). Learning and transformation take openness. In order to create or maintain that openness we will need to be uncomfortable. This is the emotional shift of the spiritual formation process. When we let go of our need for comfort we can hold on in moments of discomfort until the lesson we need to learn appears.

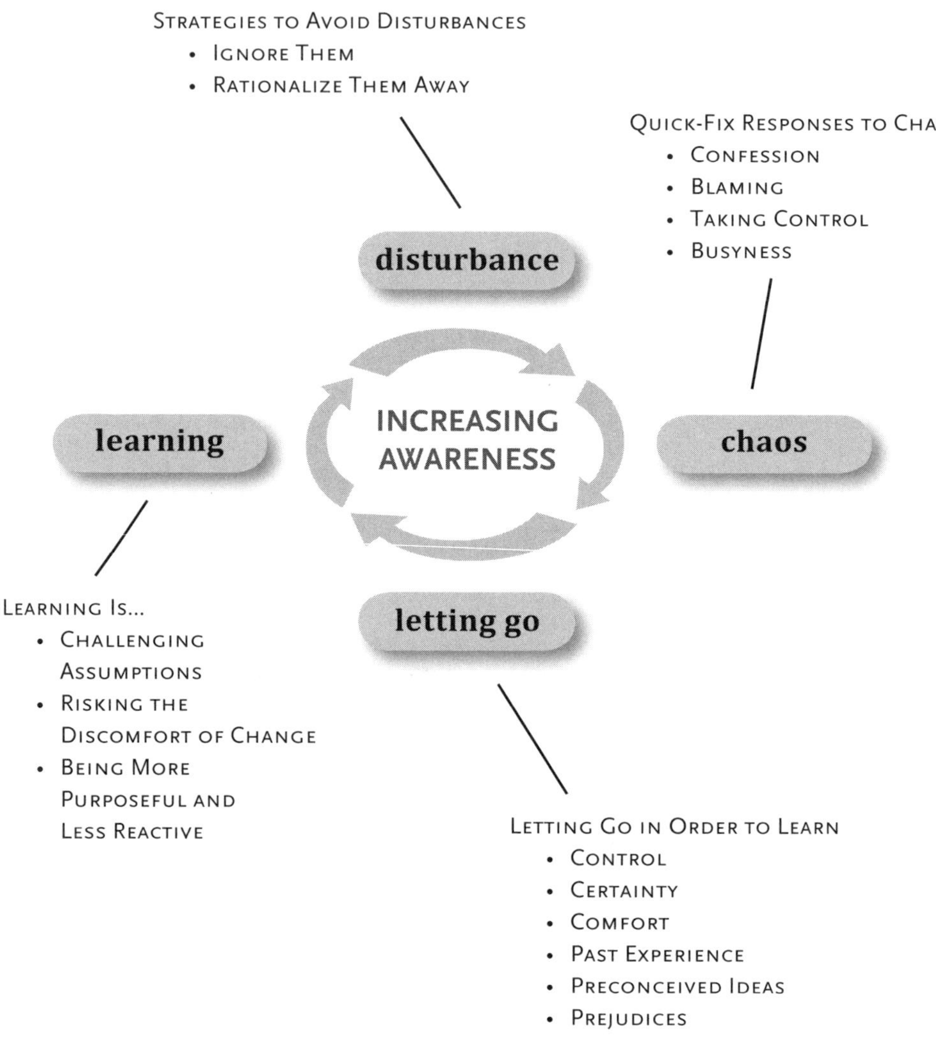

Figure 3:1

See *A Leadership Paradox: Influencing Others by Defining Yourself - Revised Edition* (2006) by Greg Robinson and Mark Rose.

5 A View of Christian Community

Community is both the product of and path to spiritual formation. A deeper spiritual life is dependent upon interaction with others and leads us to more open and inclusive relationships. Consequently, it is important for us to understand the kind of community that will lead to spiritual formation, for not all community leads us to this end.

Community was significant to the apostle John. His gospel is the only one that records Jesus' great prayer on the night of his arrest. The significant theme is that the unity of believers and their ability to love one another would be the key to the faith of others. Later, John wrote the first of three letters. Reflecting on this letter, I realized that it gives us a good foundation for creating the type of community that Jesus encouraged. This is the type of community that promotes and sustains spiritual formation.

Truth Telling

John begins with the foundation that all experts on teams, organizations, communities, and relationships come back to—trust. Trust is established in communities when people tell the truth. In my mind, this is more than not lying, but includes the willingness of people to listen with respect, to take responsibility for themselves, and to seek to be authentic. John puts it this way:

> *If we claim that we experience a shared life with him and continue to stumble around in the dark, we're obviously lying*

through our teeth—we're not living what we claim. But if we walk in the light, God himself being the light, we also experience a shared life with one another, as the sacrificed blood of Jesus, God's Son, purges all our sin.

If we claim that we're free of sin, we're only fooling ourselves. A claim like that is errant nonsense. On the other hand, if we admit our sins—make a clean breast of them—he won't let us down; he'll be true to himself. He'll forgive our sins and purge us of all wrongdoing. If we claim that we've never sinned, we out-and-out contradict God... (I John 1:6-10, The Message).

My tendency is to mistake this passage for a statement about purity. I and many who have taught me have used this passage to focus on cleaning up our act. Indeed, there is a connection between knowing the truth and walking the truth, but I believe John is communicating a greater message: There must be truth and authenticity at the foundation of all our relationships for there to be real community. A great test of this for any group or community is to observe how honest, transparent, and supportive the public conversations are among its members. My experience has been that the last place you want to tell the truth about your worries, questions, or failures is in church. As soon as you do, the responses you are likely to receive are well-meaning but misplaced efforts to fix, heal, or convert you. Our focus on being right prevents us from respecting, honoring, and supporting those who are trying to understand why they may say one thing but live another. Paul acknowledges this about himself in Romans chapter 7. I have come to believe that in starting his letter this way, John had something different in mind than always appearing pure and right.

The boundaries that John sets that provide security in this matter of truth-telling are as follows. If we say one thing and live in a way that contradicts our beliefs, then we are simply fooling ourselves and lying to the community. If we say that we have no sin or that we have never sinned, we are also being false and calling God a liar. But what lies in the middle is the real work that we each need to do to develop our spirits. We must tell the truth about our limitations, fears, and failings. The goal is not to be perfect; it is to be honest and authentic. If I am honest with myself and own my mistakes, then I am in the position to experience what I have always had, God's forgiveness. He will not force this on

The goal is not to be perfect; it is to be honest and authentic.

me. It is there but it is only accessible when we quit trying to prove ourselves and simply accept it as the gift it is.

I was about 27 years old when I first witnessed this. I was a facilitator at the time, and we had a group that participated in an adventure program. On this particular week, the activity was an introspective exercise where I had each person look into a mirror and tell the group what he or she saw. I asked them to look beyond the obvious things like eyes, noses, and the color of their hair and to look beneath the surface. We agreed that as people told the group what they saw, the group could ask questions to better understand and they could communicate their feelings to the person, but they could not attempt to fix the person. A couple of people had spoken when we came to the newest member of the group. This young lady appeared on the outside to be very together and happy. When it was her turn, she broke down into tears. She was feeling so much pressure from being a competitive dancer that she felt fake. She was tired. She felt like she was throwing away her life because she was so deep in this activity that both she and her family loved. She felt trapped. The result of her revelation and those of the other members was that they all agreed that this was the safest place they had ever experienced.

I believe this illustrates the intent behind John's opening chapter. When we tell the truth and seek to understand, clarify, and support those in our communities, we create safe places. We create places where people can be themselves without fear of judgment. There is a common humility that recognizes that we each have our struggles and no one is better than the next.

> WHEN WE TELL THE TRUTH AND SEEK TO UNDERSTAND, CLARIFY, AND SUPPORT THOSE IN OUR COMMUNITIES, WE CREATE SAFE PLACES.

Telling the truth is so important because if we are to own our true identities in God, we must be able to take a real and honest look at the identities that already control us. We will never change our basic assumptions about who we are, who God is, or how the world is until we have the courage to acknowledge, reveal, and discuss the real assumptions that we are holding at this minute. Although the truth is not my honesty, my honesty is required to see how close or how far from the truth I really am. And we cannot do that when we are a part of communities that pressure us to conform rather than be honest; when we are coerced to confirm rather than question; when we are forced to pretend rather than be authentic.

Although the truth is not my honesty, my honesty is required to see how close or how far from the truth I really am.

Spiritual formation calls us to ask difficult and challenging questions. We cannot do this well on our own. We need to come into contact with the questions and answers of others who are also seeking to develop. We cannot do this when we are constantly battling our fear of judgment, banishment, and reprisal for telling the truth.

A Real Counter-Culture

In the second chapter of John's first letter, he begins with a warning about loving the "world."

> *Don't love the world's ways. Don't love the world's goods. Love of the world squeezes out love for the Father. Practically everything that goes on in the world—wanting your own way, wanting everything for yourself, wanting to appear important—has nothing to do with the Father. It just isolates you from him. The world and all its wanting, wanting, wanting is on the way out—but whoever does what God wants is set for eternity* (I John 2:15-17, The Message).

I have most often heard this passage presented in terms of doing bad things. Yet, many faith communities in history strived for moral purity and still missed the boat in terms of really helping promote spiritual maturity. So I am offering as a starting place that we recognize that sinful actions have negative consequences for us, but if we are to build communities that promote spiritual formation, we must acknowledge that "not loving the world's ways" encompasses far more than just forsaking sex, drugs, and rock and roll. The other ways that we miss the mark can be just as damaging if not more.

I believe that John is talking about forsaking the way the "world" understands life. If we are to really forsake the world then we would do well to reconsider how we use power, make decisions, and share influence in the communities we build.

The place to begin this endeavor is to stop and really consider the system of which we are all a part. The world's system is built on the twin pillars of control and certainty.

> *Mystery surrounds every deep experience of the human heart: the deeper we go into the heart's darkness or its light, the closer we get to the ultimate mystery of God. But our culture wants to turn mysteries into puzzles to be explained or problems to be solved, because maintaining the illusion that we can 'straighten things out' makes us feel powerful* (Palmer, 2000, p. 60).

This is the dark side of the church's focus on morality. By focusing on behavior and the compliance to various lists of dos and don'ts, we are not just trying to better ourselves. Morality is a way to maintain control and certainty. It makes it easy to tell who is in and who is out. Morality makes it easy to focus on things that we can control, and the more certain we are that we are right, the further we often are from the truth.

Communities that really want to offer a different culture would do well to listen closely to the stories of Peter* on the beach or Thomas in the post-resurrection meeting with Jesus.** What makes the message of Jesus so different from all other religious schemes and their associated "rules for living life" is that the life of Jesus is squarely centered in the person of God. This is the same person who acted on our behalf before we even knew that we needed it (Romans 5:8). It is the person who reconciled us as friends even as we were still enemies (Colossians 1:20-22). It is God who has always put reconciliation ahead of retribution. Many of our communities are so busy trying to control each other with our particular descriptions of what God wants, that we have no room for trust, authenticity, and truth-telling. We are trapped in the need to appear "right" for the sake of our place in the community. We must rediscover what Paul described in Ephesians as the mystery.*** We must learn to trust what we cannot see or even explain—namely, that God has always loved us and always will. He did not try to force us to respond because the mystery of trust is that it must be chosen.

> God has always put reconciliation ahead of retribution.

If we can place our faith in the person of God rather than our performance, our communities will take on a different tone. We will

---

*John 22
**John 20:24-29
***Ephesians 3:4-6

If we can place our faith in the person of God rather than our performance, our communities will take on a different tone.

be able to listen to the deep and often profound struggles of our neighbors without the need to judge (an act of certainty) or fix (an act of control) them. We will create a safe place that is not driven by the utilitarian view of value that is so ingrained in the world. Moral transformation is the by-product of the life of faith, not the path to the life of faith.

God at the Story's Center

John has a very interesting passage that he places right in the middle of this letter.

> *My dear children, let's not just talk about love; let's practice real love. This is the only way we'll know we're living truly, living in God's reality. It's also the way to shut down debilitating self-criticism, even when there is something to it. For God is greater than our worried hearts and knows more about us than we do ourselves. And friends, once that's taken care of and we're no longer accusing or condemning ourselves, we're bold and free before God! We're able to stretch our hands out and receive...* (1 John 3:18-22, The Message).

In many Christian communities, people are caught in a difficult double bind. They are led to believe that cleaning up their lives is the most important thing, and so they focus on themselves and their behavior in order to do better. John reminds us here, however, that the more we focus on reforming ourselves, the less capable we are of receiving from God. Yet, people who focus more on knowing God and less on reforming themselves, run the risk of being considered unspiritual and marginalized by their communities.

Spiritual formation is dependent upon our willingness to encounter mystery and to trust beyond what we can know, prove, and explain.

I think the solution to this must be in moving beyond what we can rationalize to trusting what is mystery. Spiritual formation is dependent upon our willingness to encounter mystery and to trust beyond what we can prove and explain. "Scripture is not the answer book to all our problems but a doorway into the world of God's mystery" (Dawn, Peterson & Santucci, 2000, p. 69).

Accepting mystery is a terrific arena for maturing spiritually. It challenges us to encounter what we do not fully understand. This increases our capacity for emotional discomfort, and that enables us to be more patient with others and deal with the most important things in building community. Accepting mystery allows us to practice growing a faith that is not built on what we can control and explain, but on what we choose to accept and trust. If we are to really know who we are, we must be willing to hear and trust the God who tells us of our value regardless of what we can see, feel, touch, or explain.

This wrestling with the unknown deepens our humility. "It takes considerable humility to embrace this mystery, for in the presence of mystery we are not in a position to control anything, to predict or manage, to pose as authorities..." (Peterson & Dawn, 2000, p. 69). Humility keeps us open to others and enables us to build healthy communities. Some of the most important lessons of my life come from situations and people that I would never have predicted.

Perhaps most importantly, embracing the mystery of our own forgiveness despite our imperfections keeps us from developing privileged classes and protects the mutuality that community requires. When we put ourselves at the center of the story, we will inevitably begin to create divisions and classes based on who gets it, who is in and who is out, who can teach and who should learn. When we put God at the center of the story we are constantly focusing our communities back to the fact that we are all recipients of an unexplainable grace. We will help each other continue to listen to and for the Voice of acceptance. We will hear each other and not require from others what they cannot or will not give. We will remain turned toward the source of our identity, the God who knows us as we are.

When we put God at the center of the story we are constantly focusing our communities back to the fact that we are all recipients of an unexplainable grace.

Without Fear

When communities tell the stories of mystery with the right character at the center they become places with much less fear. This is also a criterion we can use to assess the health and maturity of our communities. "The core message of all the great spiritual traditions is 'Be not afraid'" (Palmer, 1990). It is also the core message with which John ends his letter.

> *God is love. When we take up permanent residence in a life of love, we live in God and God lives in us. This way love has the run of the house, becomes at home and mature in us, so that we're free of worry on Judgment Day—our standing in the world is identical with Christ's. There is no room in love for fear. Well-formed love banishes fear. Since fear is crippling, a fearful life—fear of death, fear of judgment—is one not fully formed in love* (1 John 4:16-18, The Message).

There was a time in my life when the sight of a church or being inside one brought me a sense of profound importance and safety. Unfortunately, after years of work and life in ill-formed communities of faith, I now have the exact opposite experience. I tense up. I fade against the nearest wall or quickly move to the nearest seat and wither away into the margin. I do not feel church is a safe place. This is not the community John had in mind when writing his letter.

Taking a risk in the company of trusted friends is much different than taking risks in a company of strangers.

Communities without fear are not places of permanent bliss, life does not work that way. John is telling us is that they should be places where people do not fear condemnation, judgment, or ridicule. Embracing mystery and risking trust will always include some apprehension. Yet taking a risk in the company of trusted friends is much different than taking risks in a company of strangers.

This is the culmination of all that has been discussed so far. Communities without fear tell the truth. They hope for the future. They tackle important but difficult problems. They listen first and embrace more freely. They hear people where they are without strings, agendas, or requirements. When we can listen without judgment, we will hear our own pain, calling us to cast off illusions that have done a poor job of imitating life. There is room for all who dare to find their true identities. Members of such a place help each other remember the truth. When there is doubt about our state of acceptance, communities without fear remind us of what we cannot remember for ourselves—that we are loved and accepted.

6 A Particular Kind of Teaching

The kind of learning that encompasses spiritual formation requires a particular kind of teaching. Specifically, it requires that we learn from our experiences. Experiential learning and facilitation have two basic elements: action and reflection. Action is the practice of living. If we seek to grow spiritually but only think, we risk an illusionary faith. We can become certain about what we think we believe, but deep down, live what we truly believe. Action will keep us honest. Each day we live what we believe. We never do anything that does not reflect what we truly believe. Our behavior and responses may not line up with what we think we believe, but they always reflect what we truly believe. As Margaret Silf (1999) says, "We do not make choices that we do not choose." So for the spiritual facilitator, this inconsistency is simply a fact to be aware of and the response is to be with people as they act, do, go, and work. We are to watch and observe, waiting for the opportunity to understand more clearly the people around us.

The flip side of experiential learning is reflection. Many of us have experiences that we do not learn from. We act each day and our filtering mechanisms see those things that confirm our intentions and beliefs, while dismissing our inconsistencies. We can live our entire lives asleep to the assumptions and beliefs that shape us. Reflection—intentional reflection—is the discipline of stopping along the way and noticing what our actions

We can live our entire lives asleep to the assumptions and beliefs that shape us.

and emotions are telling us about ourselves. It is the practice of making sense of the world and relationships in which we live.

Close Proximity

There is no doubt that among the many things Jesus was, he was a great teacher. He was able in 3 years to effectively change the belief system and behavior patterns of an incredibly diverse group of people. I firmly believe that at the foundation of his teaching was a use of experiences. As we follow Jesus through alleyways, saloons, synagogues, and relationships, we hear him talk of common things. His messages were based on ordinary experiences that everyone could relate to. There were times, with his 12 closest followers, that he structured experiences to teach them. At least two different times, He sent them two by two into villages to practice what they had seen and heard from him (Luke 9 & 10). Upon their return, he listened and talked with them concerning their experiences. The feeding of the 5,000 was a definite learning experience for his faithless followers.* The raising of Lazarus greatly impacted those who were there.** These examples of Jesus' experiential teaching reveal some of the benefits for both the teacher and the pupil.

> *As soon as the meal was finished, he insisted that the disciples get in the boat and go to the other side while he dismissed the people. With the crowd dispersed, he climbed the mountain so he could be by himself and pray. He stayed there alone, late into the night. Meanwhile, the boat was far out to sea when the wind came up against them and they were battered by the waves. At about four o'clock in the morning, Jesus came toward them walking on the water. They were scared out of their wits. "A ghost!" they said, crying out in terror. But Jesus was quick to comfort them. "Courage, it's me. Don't be afraid." Peter, suddenly bold, said, "Master, if it's really you, call me to come to you on the water." He said, "Come ahead." Jumping out of the boat, Peter walked on the water to Jesus. But when he looked down at the waves churning beneath his feet, he lost his nerve and started to sink. He cried, "Master,*

---

* Matthew 14:15-21
** John 11

save me!" Jesus didn't hesitate. He reached down and grabbed his hand. Then he said, "Faint-heart, what got into you?" The two of them climbed in the boat, and the wind died down. The disciples in the boat, having watched the whole thing, worshipped Jesus, saying, "This is it! You are God's Son for sure!" (MATTHEW 14:22-34)

It is not often that a teacher has such a great setup for a lesson. This circumstance contains all the elements that are needed for a true teaching moment. There was definitely stress in the situation. The hearts of these 12 men were pumping wildly in the midst of the storm. That near panic escalated 100 percent when they looked up from their bailing to see a man walking across the water. There was also a challenge issued. Peter was definitely questioning his abilities in this new experience when he called from the boat, asking to stroll upon the waves himself. Beyond the circumstances (stress and challenging task) and of equal importance was the fact that a capable teacher was present. As Peter stepped into the unknown chaos of the storm and sea, he had choices to make. What he truly believed surfaced—his faith was weak and his water-walking skills were inept. These shortcomings did not lead to the disaster they could have, because Jesus was there to step in as Peter found himself in over his head.

THE REAL SHORTCOMING OF RELIGIOUS EDUCATION IS THAT IT MOST OFTEN TAKES PLACE SO FAR AWAY FROM REAL-LIFE SITUATIONS.

This is the **first major advantage of experiential learning. As pupils are making their choices and acting upon those choices, the teacher is there to have immediate influence on the situation.** The real shortcoming of religious education is that it most often takes place so far away from real-life situations. A situation that is talked about on Sunday may not take place for days, weeks, or even months. Consequently, by the time the student is most in need of direction, he or she is farthest from the teacher. Church leaders rarely find out about possibly difficult or dangerous situations until the damage is already done. Experiential learning uses real situations, actual group dynamics, and personal choices to teach awareness as these things occur. Had Jesus been waiting for Peter to come to class on Sunday to talk about his experience, Peter would have been out of luck. Processing an experience as it is happening and is fresh in the

EXPERIENTIAL LEARNING USES REAL SITUATIONS, ACTUAL GROUP DYNAMICS, AND PERSONAL CHOICES TO TEACH AWARENESS AS THESE THINGS OCCUR.

minds of everyone allows for more powerful learning. It also limits the long-term damage caused by making wrong decisions.

Honest Responses

> *Late that day he said to them, "Let's go across to the other side." They took him in the boat as he was. Other boats came along. A huge storm came up. Waves poured into the boat, threatening to sink it. And Jesus was in the stern, head on a pillow, sleeping! They roused him, saying, 'Teacher, is it nothing to you that we're going to drown?" Awake now, he told the wind to pipe down and said to the sea, "Quiet! Settle down!" The wind ran out of breath; the sea became smooth as glass. Jesus reprimanded the disciples: "Why are you such cowards? Don't you have any faith at all?" They were in absolute awe, staggered. "Who is this, anyway?" they asked. "Wind and sea at his beck and call!"* (MARK 4:35-41, THE MESSAGE)

One thing I have learned in life is that people rarely speak what is truly on their minds. Most of us are afraid to be totally honest with any except those closest to us, and then it is often a struggle. Most of the answers we get are what people think we want to hear. Usually this is not a conscious deception. People want to be liked and they understand the human mind in that all of us like to be agreed with. Consequently, people spend much of their energy trying to guess what we want to hear.

> MOST OF THE ANSWERS WE GET ARE WHAT PEOPLE THINK WE WANT TO HEAR.

I think it was the same with Jesus and his disciples. They asked him questions. They watched him perform numerous signs. They listened to his stories. In the end, however, they did not speak of their deepest doubts. That is, until experience forced them into moments of honesty and vulnerability. This boat ride was such a moment. I have often wondered why Jesus was so angry with the disciples. It only makes sense that these men would be frightened in a storm that was threatening to sink their boat. How could Jesus criticize them for this natural reaction? I believe Jesus' words came from a deep realization of an underlying belief about him rather than at how the men were responding to the storm. His accusation of cowardice was because these men still did not trust him. In this very real moment of stress and challenge what they really believed about Jesus came pouring out. They did not believe he really cared for them. Instead of asking him for help, they assumed the worst. They assumed he would rather let them drown than be awakened from his nap.

Although this was a difficult moment in the lives of all involved, true learning was happening. The disciples revealed what was in their hearts. Jesus, on the other hand, was able to respond to their doubts in the midst of their doubting. I have no doubt that these men remembered that moment for the rest of their lives. **Another of the wonderful benefits of experiential learning is that it often elicits honest and vulnerable responses.** This happens because all of the person is engaged in the learning experience. Participants simply react without giving thought to the political correctness of their reaction. These are some of the most precious times between student and teacher. We react on the basis of what we truly believe and know to be true. Just like an athlete reacts in the midst of the action based on how he or she has practiced, we react in life based on what we believe about ourselves, others, and God. We rarely get these kinds of reactions and honesty in a classroom. This is true because we have not engaged the whole person. We are playing intellectual games or partaking in intellectual exercises. This type of interaction makes it too easy to disengage and cover up our true feelings and beliefs. Only when the learning experience realistically parallels life do we get into the deepest beliefs of others.

ONLY WHEN THE LEARNING EXPERIENCE REALISTICALLY PARALLELS LIFE DO WE GET INTO THE DEEPEST BELIEFS OF OTHERS.

Jesus practiced experiential learning. He used real and structured experiences to teach his disciples. These teaching experiences allowed him to get to the deepest doubts and beliefs of his students. These experiences allowed him to accompany his followers as they were making choices and learning, thus giving him the opportunity to step in and help when needed. Ministry is much more powerful when we place ourselves as spiritual facilitators in the actual experiences of our students and allow them to share their most honest thoughts and feelings. Because we cannot follow our students most of the time, we need to purposefully structure activities that reflect real-life situations. The answer is to create real tasks and experiences that are challenging and fun. When everyone is engaged, real, long-term learning can be seen.

7 The Spiritual Facilitator

The Mindset of the Facilitator

Perhaps the most challenging work of the process of spiritual formation is for those of us who want to facilitate the formation process with others. The challenge we face is not one of getting the right information or the right techniques, but of getting beyond our need to be essential. If anything will sidetrack our ability to be of assistance, it will be our need to help, to get things done, and to provide direction. The key word in the sentence above is "need." Spiritual formation is a lifelong process of stripping away the illusions that we use to prop ourselves up in this world. So the spiritual facilitator's mindset must be one of helping people see those illusions or "needs" and it must start within the facilitator. Consequently, the foundational mindset of the facilitator is hospitality, which is only possible when we let go of our need for control and certainty.

> The challenge we face is not one of getting the right information or the right techniques, but of getting beyond our need to be essential.

"I think the most powerful protest against destruction is the laying bare of the basis of all destructiveness: the illusion of control" (Nouwen, 2005, p. 41). There is a common activity in the experiential learning field in which a group of people are asked to lay a tent pole or hula hoop on the ground. The interesting thing about this activity is how much time participants spend doing the opposite of what they intend. For most of the early moments of the activity include a steady and sometimes rapid raising of the pole while the entire group is saying, "go down." The paradoxical truth about this activity is that as soon as they can collectively stop trying to lower the pole, the pole will go down on its own. Why? Because when members are trying to lay the pole down, there is too much intent, though often unconscious, to be in control. Group members are so busy trying to prove themselves and take control of the group, they fail to realize it is their own persistence in trying to "not lose contact" that promotes as much of the failure as the people they are trying to correct.

The same is true for the spiritual facilitator. The more we try to fix, heal, convert, and in a sense, control the formation of others, the more damage we do. The spiritual facilitator's job is not to get people to be a certain way or even to do a certain thing. We are to watch, listen, and provide structure when needed, but we must be comfortable with letting God and our participants find their way together even if that way is a way that we do not understand. I think this passage from Henri Nouwen frames it very nicely:

Activity Instructions:

1. Divide the group into two parallel lines facing each other.
2. Have them lift their arms and extend their index fingers, making a zipper out of alternating fingers. You should end up with a straight line of fingers, waist high, between the two lines.
3. The objective is for the group to lay the tent pole that will be placed on their fingers on the ground. Give them the following guidelines:
    - They cannot just pull their fingers out and let the pole drop. It must be laid on the ground.
    - They cannot place their fingers on top of the pole, pinch the pole or hook it with their fingers. The pole must stay at rest on top of their fingers.
    - Finally, they cannot lose contact with the pole. If anyone does, the group must start over.
4. Blindfolds are optional.

(I learned this activity from Mike Gass.)

WE MUST BE COMFORTABLE WITH LETTING GOD AND OUR PARTICIPANTS FIND THEIR WAY TOGETHER.

Hospitality, therefore, means primarily the creating of a free space where the stranger can enter and become a friend instead of an enemy. Hospitality is not to change people, but to offer them space where change can take place. It is not to bring men and women over to our side, but to offer freedom not disturbed by dividing lines. It is not to lead our neighbor into a corner where there are no alternatives left, but to open a wide spectrum of options for choice and commitment. It is not an educated intimidation with good books, good stories, and good works, but the liberation of fearful hearts so that words can find roots and bear ample fruit. It is not a method of making ... our way into the criteria of happiness, but the opening of an opportunity to others to find their own way (NOUWEN, 1975, P. 71-72).

The facilitator's mindset is one of hospitality. That hospitality is possible only when we trust in the free will of people and more importantly, the unending influence of God in our world. So we must let go of our need to be right or to be in charge. We must free ourselves of the need to always know the answers or to never be surprised. We must let go of all our inclinations to believe that we are essential to the formation process. We can participate and we can even be quite helpful but our willingness to wait and trust must outweigh our need to be in control.

Having said all of this, I want to leave you with what I hope is a comforting thought. One of my favorite stories in the Old Testament is the story of Jonah* because it reminds me of God's great safety net. You see, in the story, Jonah never gets it right. He starts by running, setting his own course, being in control of his life. When that doesn't work, he goes and does the work he is supposed to do only to end up angry and pouting when he is in fact successful. God wanted him to preach to the people of Nineveh. Jonah did and they repented, much to Jonah's dismay. The moral of the story for me is that God's work is indeed bigger than me. Even when I get it wrong or am not aware of doing anything at all, He is at work. I can trust that even if I don't understand it.

---

*Jonah 1-4

Roles: Prophet, Priest, and Facilitator

Prophets and priests have always played important but unique roles in God's story of earth. It is beneficial to the spiritual facilitator to know about these roles.

The prophet has two very important jobs. **First, the prophet is the one who is willing to tell the honest truth about what is, no matter how uncomfortable that truth may be.** The prophet holds up the mirror to societies, villages, and individuals to reflect their current state. The same is true for the spiritual facilitator. The facilitator needs to pay attention and reflect back to the person or group what they are doing, hoping to get to the assumptions that may be discovered by looking at the participants' actions. Many of us need help seeing our part in things or the blind spots that exist between our intentions and our actions. The curious but persistent exploration of participants' actions, moods, and responses is critical to waking them up to the spiritual formation process.

Prophets also stretch the imagination of the people as to what could be. Prophets must be courageous, unafraid of reaching far to promote a potential future state. People often have difficulty clarifying their hopes, seeing their potential, and articulating their dreams and callings. Prophets help that process by broadcasting what is possible in God's great story. The spiritual facilitator stretches his or her participants' minds concerning what is possible in terms of honesty, self-awareness, compassion, and trust. The prophet lures us into a dangerous encounter with God's action. Prophets and good facilitators always look beyond what is obvious to see what lies beneath our fearful facades.

PROPHETS AND GOOD FACILITATORS ALWAYS LOOK BEYOND WHAT IS OBVIOUS TO SEE WHAT LIES BENEATH OUR FEARFUL FACADES.

The priest has a different job. It is not as glamorous as the prophet. The prophet stirs things up and continues on to the next venue, but the priest lives among the people for the longterm. Priests are keepers of the Story. Their rituals remember and retell the great story of God's action for us as well as the small stories of our encounters with that story and each other. **The important work of the priest is to help us find and keep our place in the Story so that we can remember who we are.** Among all the voices clamoring to tell us our worth, our value, our purpose—there is the priest faithfully calling us to distinguish between these voices until we here the Voice of the Truth. So it is for the spiritual facilitator. In the midst of challenging experiences, many voices rise to give us direction. The facilitator helps us listen between the lines, consider any illusions that need to be revealed, and continue to ask good and important questions.

Presence

Perhaps the most important role of the facilitator is just to be present. Every journey of spiritual formation is a personal one. There may be milestones or touch points that give some common indication of where a person is along the journey, but the path will always be unique. It is easy for the facilitator to try to get everyone onto the same road he or she traveled. Here the landscape is familiar and the challenges are predictable. But that is not the work of the facilitator. The effective facilitator chooses to join the journey and live among the people as they try to discern their way forward. This is no small role though it is perhaps an unexpected role. The effective facilitator realizes that he or she is not the keeper of the map, but rather an expert in traveling. The facilitator is not a GPS system telling people which way to go, but rather someone who has some experience with destinations. Facilitators may not always know the way, but they do try to keep in mind the characteristics of progress and some idea of the quality of the final destination. In times of great uncertainty, facilitators can lend courage, patience, and persistence to pilgrims who, along the journey, lose their grip on such things.

PERHAPS THE MOST IMPORTANT ROLE OF THE FACILITATOR IS JUST TO BE PRESENT.

Let me tell a story that illustrates the point I am trying to make. Many years ago a group of high school and junior high students arrived at their local Methodist church only to be presented with a dilemma. I told them that inside their classroom were the secrets to God and life. The only problem was that all the doors were locked, so they would have to find a way in. The only parameters that I gave them were that they could not destroy anything nor could they ask anyone for the key. As I sat observing their progress, I noticed many traits that people on an adventure have in common. Some quit and chose for others to lead them. Some experimented with unlocking the door, excitedly using trial and error in hopes of discovering the passage. Others sought to understand the entire situation, thinking broad and wide about the possibilities, which, in the end, paid off. They discovered that the windows in the old building not only lifted up, but the tops pulled down, and in that way, they entered the room. It was a curious and revealing lesson for all of us.

As the facilitator, what did I do to help them? I gave no answers, hints, or suggestions. I did, however, remain among them. If I had gone for coffee, I fear they would have lost heart or gotten distracted because of the difficulty of the test. But by being among them, communicating my confidence that there was a solution and they were capable of finding it, the focus and motivation that was needed by those who were truly searching was provided. I think also, a second lesson that I learned is that I cannot force my way on them. I had left them a way into the room, which was only fair. Yet, it was not this entrance that they discovered but another one wholly unknown to me. If I had tried to tell them the one way, we would never have learned of other options.

THE CHALLENGE FOR THE FACILITATOR IS TO AVOID BECOMING DISTRACTED OR DISCOURAGED BY THE PACE OF THE SEARCH.

The presence of the facilitator is of highest importance. It is often the difference between the person or group quitting or continuing forward. It is difficult work, waiting until people find their way to a crossroads—decision points where they are ready to consider new questions. The challenge for the facilitator is to avoid becoming distracted or discouraged by the pace of the search. It is not the spiritual facilitator's role to determine if people are journeying fast enough, only to accompany them in their way, offering support and companionship.

Questions

Finally, a key role for the facilitator is to ask questions. If a spiritual facilitator is going to be successful with questions, there are some things that must be recognized. Questions are a double-edged sword. Used one way, we develop mature people who think for themselves. Used another, we kill all tendency to learn. What is the difference?

A KEY ROLE FOR THE FACILITATOR IS TO ASK QUESTIONS.

First, never ask a question that you don't want to be answered honestly. Too often questions are asked, not for the answer but as a way to elicit a response we want others to have. If one is successful in that strategy, only dishonesty and suppression of our true thoughts is taught. Asking questions is a place where real trust is either built or destroyed. As a facilitator, I strive to ask only the questions that I want to hear answered honestly, and I work very hard at not being shocked by those answers. Two things are accomplished by guarding my responses to the shocking answers. The person or group's confidence in the facilitator grows as they realize that the facilitator is not secretly sitting in judgment on them. And it also tends to eliminate answers from people who have no interest in mutual trust but whose intention is control or attention.

Secondly, ask questions that are open, not leading. Teachers, who tend to ask leading questions, ask them in such a way that the answer that is sought is given in the question. Used in this way, questions continue to narrow options until the "right" answer emerges. Again, participants are taught not to think for themselves. On occasions when a person will not be corralled, the facilitator can find himself pinned in a hole with no way out. Conversation stops and the facilitator loses credibility, or things devolve into a debate, which is a contest of wills. No one wins in this scenario.

Conclusion

How we facilitate will have more impact on our students than what we teach. Years later, almost no one remembers the content of a lesson, but they do remember the method and the intent. I know for myself, I look back on those I consider most influential in my life and I remember very little of the content that they taught me. What I do remember is their attitude toward me and the relationship that was established.

How we facilitate will have more impact on our students than what we teach.

8 The Containers of Formation

If spiritual formation is God's work in us, what is our role as spiritual facilitators and teachers? I suggest that a key role for us is to create containers of formation. A container is a defined place, time frame, or experience that is set aside to intentionally explore something. A container is not the work, but rather a context that makes it easier for us to wake up and attend to the work already being done. Spiritual formation does take some focus in terms of prayer, reflection, community, and listening. Containers are places which enable us to build some greater ability in these practical matters of spiritual formation. I have found retreat, pilgrimage and service to be three especially effective containers.

Retreat

> RETREAT – A NOVEL SETTING THAT REQUIRES US TO CHANGE OUR NORMAL PACE OF LIFE.

"Next Jesus was taken into the wild by the Spirit for the Test" (Matthew 4:1, *The Message*). I find it interesting that the first thing Jesus did after the public initiation of his baptism was go on retreat. He went to the wilderness for 40 days for the Test. What was the test? The same test that we take when we fully enter into retreat, namely, considering whose voice we will trust. Henri Nouwen (1989) in his book *In the Name of Jesus*, describes this test as Jesus having to face and decide the kind of person and Savior he would be. Would he listen to the voice from his baptism, "This is my beloved Son, chosen and marked by my love, delight of my life," or would he succumb to the temptations to be spectacular, relevant, and powerful? The nature of our search and reflection are very much the same. Our temptations may not be to turn stones to bread,* but we are tempted to take charge of life and make things happen by the force of our will. Retreat is an ideal place to face ourselves and hear the truth. In retreat, we can listen to and come to trust the voice that says to us, "This is my beloved child, in whom I am well pleased."

What makes retreat effective? Why is it such a good container for spiritual formation? I think it is because retreat drastically changes our context and the pace of activity. I have become convinced that place and context are very important parts of waking up and growing our spirits. Having grown up in the evangelical church world, I noticed that place, space, and setting were always moved to the back in favor of ideas and answers. Yet, we need from time to time, to come into contact with not only people we don't know but also places that we do not know. The encounter with a setting that is very different from our daily routine brings both a curiosity and a sense of disequilibrium as we try to figure out where we are, how we feel about it, and what our place in it should be. Some places are considered sacred because others have come into contact with God there in a different way. These are like the "thin places" of Celtic tradition. Some are just different from what we know. I love visiting new cities. I currently live in Oklahoma, and I have lived nearly all of my life in rural settings. When I get a chance to visit Boston, Seattle, or New Orleans, I always come away with a unique feeling. It does not matter what I am doing, it matters where I am. The architecture, the natural setting of mountain or ocean, even the distinctive accents bring a new spirit of exploration to me. This is the work of retreat. We step out of that which is familiar to encounter something we have not known or at least have not paid attention to. Setting can do this. The further away we are from what we know, the more powerful the setting can be.

THE ENCOUNTER WITH A SETTING THAT IS VERY DIFFERENT FROM OUR DAILY ROUTINE BRINGS BOTH A CURIOSITY AND A SENSE OF DISEQUILIBRIUM AS WE TRY TO FIGURE OUT WHERE WE ARE, HOW WE FEEL ABOUT IT, AND WHAT OUR PLACE IN IT SHOULD BE.

---

*Matthew 4:1-4

A second element is the pace of time. Generally, retreat will include some elements of solitude. Often the word "retreat" is used to describe an outing, where all the time is filled with activities. That is not retreat. Retreat is meant to help us slow down in order to hear what we are generally too busy to notice.

> Retreat is meant to help us slow down in order to hear what we are generally too busy to notice.

> *In solitude, we can listen to the voice of him who spoke to us before we could speak a word, who healed us before we could make any gesture to help, who set us free long before we could free others, and who loved us long before we could give love to anyone. It is in this solitude that we discover that being is more important than having, and that we are worth more than the result of our efforts. In solitude, we discover that our life is not a possession to be defended, but a gift to be shared* (Nouwen, 1974, p. 22).

This type of setting and pace can be threatening and even frightening. We do not like the unknown and we like being alone even less. Being alone presents too many opportunities to have to pay attention to our lives, our fears, our relationships, and our choices. We can hear what the din of technology and entertainment often cover up.

> *In solitude I get rid of my scaffolding; no friends to talk with, no telephone calls to make, no meetings to attend, no music to entertain, no books to distract, just me—naked, vulnerable, weak, sinful, deprived, broken—nothing. It is this nothingness that I have to face in my solitude, a nothingness so dreadful that everything in me wants to run to my friends, my work, and my distractions so that I can forget my nothingness and make myself believe that I am worth something* (Nouwen, 1981, p. 27).

In retreat, I am called to face myself and consider who I believe myself to be. It is the place where I will do battle with my fears and illusions. It may be a time when I experience God's concern for me regardless of the state of my perfection.

In retreat, we have a chance to encounter that which will give us the ability to love, listen to, and care for others.

When I see myself and come to trust who God says I am—without the props of position, status, accomplishment, or duty— I am finally in a place to be a real contribution to others.

...why solitude gives birth to compassion... Because it makes us die to our neighbor... in order to be of service to others we have to die to them; that is, we have to give up measuring our meaning and value with the yardstick of others. To die to our neighbors means to stop judging them, to stop evaluating them, and thus to become free to be compassionate (Nouwen, 1981, p. 34-35).

When I see myself and come to trust who God says I am—without the props of position, status, accomplishment, or duty—I am finally in a place to be a real contribution to others.

Pilgrimage

When we venture forth, we set out on a path that ultimately leads us where we need to go in order to become what we're meant to be. —Kerry Walters

Pilgrimage in its truest sense is religiously motivated travel for the purpose of meeting and experiencing God with hopes of being shaped and changed by the encounter. —Arthur Boers

Pilgrimage is physical travel with a spiritual destination. —Daniel Taylor

The work of spiritual formation is a slow business. It takes time and as we have talked about before, it takes courage and honesty. There is no container that will produce these elements together as well as pilgrimage. Pilgrims set off on journeys with an uncertain knowledge of what will happen or what the destination will be like, expecting full well to be tested along the way.

Think of it this way,... a pilgrimage is a way of praying on your feet. You go on a pilgrimage because you know there's something missing inside your soul, and the only way you can find it is to go to sacred places, places where God made himself known to others. In sacred places, something is done to you that you've been unable to do for yourself (Cron, 2006, p. 42).

So what specifically does pilgrimage offer groups and individuals that is unique to its form of container? First of all, it offers **extended time together** with a small group of people. A true pilgrimage is done on foot, although there is some of the same benefit to be found in extended road trips. When people spend such a long period of time together, the barriers and facades that they use to protect themselves and keep others at bay begin to crumble. We cannot keep up appearances for extended periods of time. Our true selves will begin to emerge over time and that is what the spiritual facilitator is counting on. The work of discovering who God says we are takes a great deal of honesty, particularly with ourselves. Extended journeys provide the unhurried time which will bring forth things we did not know about ourselves as well as things we have tried to keep hidden. The uncovering of our unmentionables scares us. Yet if we can dare to consider this we will come to understand, "The revelation of sinfulness reveals who we are, but it also reveals who God is and who he wants to be for us" (Barry, 2001, p. 51).

> WE CANNOT KEEP UP APPEARANCES FOR EXTENDED PERIODS OF TIME.

A second element of pilgrimage is **struggle**. A long walk may sound enticing on the front end, but we are no longer people of long walks. Most of us would consider a 4- or 5-mile walk a full day's work. So when we undertake a walk of 100 miles or more, where we walk 10 miles a day for 10 days or more, we realize there is real demand and struggle in the pilgrim's way. Beyond the expected pain from the physical demand of walking, there are hours of boredom and a heavy realization that nothing comes fast on the trail. You cannot jump in your car and go to the corner for what you need. Every place you go requires that much more from you. Yet, this struggle, in addition to the revelation of self and God, builds something much needed for the long walk of life—perseverance. In the walk, we learn to hang in there even if it is tough going. We learn to appreciate small things like a cool stream, a break in the clouds, or soft bed of pine needles. We also start to learn of the ever-present mystery and wonder God has built into our world. When we finally drop exhausted into bed, fully expecting that it will be days before we can take another step, we discover that during your "death" or sleep, there is health and renewal in our resurrection and awaken-

> WE TOO OFTEN DO NOT FULLY LIVE THE REALITY OF OUR RESURRECTION IDENTITIES BECAUSE WE QUIT TOO SOON.

ing. We too often do not fully live the reality of our resurrection identities because we quit too soon. We settle for what is manageable. But on the other side of the imaginable are life, freedom, and peace. We must risk the struggle to find ourselves and the compassion for others needed to complete the trip well.

Perhaps the most powerful element of pilgrimage has to do with the **emotional shift** required to start a journey into the unknown. The work of repentance,* of changing direction in the way we think and act, requires us to see things from new or different angles. This requires an emotional shift as much as it does an intellectual one. It is unnerving to contact things and people which you may not understand. It is our ability to not panic, to not react to what we don't know or control that will allow us to encounter what we need to see and understand. It is important to realize that repentance, the ability to change direction, is always initiated by God as He reveals truth to us. "Even today when the proclamations of that old, bankrupt government are read out, they can't see through it. Only Christ can get rid of the veil so they can see for themselves that there's nothing there" (2 Corinthians 3:14, *The Message*). Yet, God does not force this on us and so we are left to respond. That is our part and it is here that courage and the maturity to not panic in the face of what is new is so important. We must stay open to learning lessons even if they are hard for us. Learning to trust who God says we are requires us to die to that which we use to define ourselves. This is a death that is often faced in the midst of the pilgrim's wilderness. As Walters (2001, p. 9) reminds us, "death awaits the desert traveler, and it is both dreadful and unavoidable."

OUR ABILITY TO NOT PANIC, TO NOT REACT TO WHAT WE DON'T KNOW OR CONTROL WILL ALLOW US TO ENCOUNTER WHAT WE NEED TO SEE AND UNDERSTAND.

EXPERIENCED FAITH REQUIRES A LEARNING BEYOND INFORMATION AND STATISTICS.

This courage is something that can be developed as we face fears rather than run from them. Choosing to start a journey, when we do not fully know the path or the destination or even its impact on us, is an act of courageous intent that will develop the stamina and maturity that we all need. For we must, if we are to

*Repent, Metanoeo, to think differently. Metanoia, to reverse a decision. *Strong's Concordance.*

know who God says we are, learn how to learn in a new way. Experienced faith requires a learning beyond information and statistics.

> *The working assumption behind the koan is simple enough: If a person is ever to achieve enlightenment, she must first clear her mind and soul of all intellectual preconceptions about the nature of things. These contrivances stand between her and a naked encounter with what is. Her problem is that she knows how to think, but not how to experience. To move from one to the other, she must let go of the conceptual filters through which she habitually strains reality* (Walters, 2001, p. 4).

This requires courage, emotional awareness, and emotional stamina, as do all lessons learned through the struggle on the pilgrim's way.

Before we move on, there are two final elements that pilgrimage offers us. We live in a world of technology, entertainment, and virtual communication. Ours is a time dominated by information and the belief that education, or should I say the right information, will solve anything. Our faith work has become dominated by these same values. What we have forgotten is the power and benefit of sacrament. Sacrament is the outward expression of an unseen and inner work. Why do you think God sent Jesus in concrete form? Don't you think that He could have just given us the right answers? No, **faith is an experience that must be lived**. Pilgrimage is a place for us to walk out the inner searching of our souls. "Pilgrimage 'unites belief with action, thinking with doing' and requires that 'the body and its actions express the desires and beliefs of the soul.' Pilgrimage is about integration, body and soul, feet and faith" (Boers, 2007, p. 23). In the steps we take while walking the pilgrim's path we heal the false dichotomies that have taken root in our psyche. No longer is the doing separated from thinking, nor body from spirit. We find a faith that is rooted in our whole being rather than an illusion of faith shielded in our minds.

We find a faith that is rooted in our whole being rather than an illusion of faith shielded in our minds.

The journey of the pilgrim gives us a **time to learn to listen**. It is a liminal space (relating to a sensory threshold) that mirrors the experience of those who have not yet found their way. Young adults especially are trapped in a gap between adolescence and adulthood. "The liminal state is characterized by ambiguity, openness, and indeterminacy. One's sense of identity dissolves to some extent, bringing about disorientation. Liminality is a period of transition where normal limits to thought, self-understanding, and behavior are relaxed—a situation that can lead to new perspectives.*" On the journey, the pilgrim is released from the past and cannot yet see a future. There is only the daily routine of getting from one place to the next. Here we can learn to pay attention in a way that we normally do not. Here the voice of the One that calls us "beloved" may pierce our notice and bring life with it.

Service

The apostle John had a special fondness for service. He comes back to that theme over and over in his first letter. In fact, he tells us that the practice of love "is the only way we'll know we're living truly, living in God's reality" (I John 3:18, *The Message*). I think it is a fine container for discovering our true selves and the work of God, which is shaping those selves. But this container should come with the strongest warning because it is the most seductive of the three. Service is the easiest of the containers for us to slip back to the center of the story and attempt to take charge. Through service there is a subversive enticement to change the world by doing good for others.

> THE CONTAINER OF SERVICE SHOULD COME WITH THE STRONGEST WARNING BECAUSE WE CAN SO EASILY SLIP BACK TO THE CENTER OF THE STORY AND ATTEMPT TO TAKE CHARGE.

Some months ago, I was reflecting on this passage found at the end of Matthew's gospel.

> *When he finally arrives, blazing in beauty and all his angels with him, the Son of Man will take his place on his glorious throne. Then all the nations will be arranged before him and he will sort the people out, much as a shepherd sorts out sheep and goats, putting sheep to his right and goats to his left. Then the King will say to those on his right, "Enter, you who are blessed by my Father! Take what's coming to you in this kingdom. It's been ready for you since the world's foundation. And here's why:*

---

* http://en.wikipedia.org/wiki/Liminality

I was hungry and you fed me,
I was thirsty and you gave me a drink,
I was homeless and you gave me a room,
I was shivering and you gave me clothes,
I was sick and you stopped to visit,
I was in prison and you came to me."

Then those "sheep" are going to say, "Master, what are you talking about? When did we ever see you hungry and feed you, thirsty and give you a drink? And when did we ever see you sick or in prison and come to you?" Then the King will say, "I'm telling the solemn truth: Whenever you did one of these things to someone overlooked or ignored, that was me—you did it to me" (Matthew 25:31-40, The Message).

It occurred to me like a blind man seeing for the first time how strange a story this really is. There is a genuine naiveté to those identified as righteous. How could they not know they were doing the right thing? I think it is because all of the responses listed by Jesus were natural responses to others out of relationship. They did not plan these actions as a mission or strategically decide how to use their time and resources. They simply responded to people in need that they knew and did what a compassionate person would do. They helped someone who needed help. There was no bigger agenda. If we create the service container well, there will be a similar natural response rather than a well-planned program.

If we create the service container well, there will be a natural response rather than a well-planned program.

So the question for the spiritual facilitator is how do we protect this container so that it does not become tainted by our own ambition? I think three considerations can provide some protection—relationship, a correct understanding of compassion, and being open to being taught by the poor. I want to start with compassion.

Compassion means to become close to the one who suffers. But we can come close to another person only when we are willing to become vulnerable ourselves. A compassionate person says: "I am your brother; I am your sister; I am human, fragile, and mortal, just like you. I am not scandalized by your tears, nor afraid of your pain. I too have wept. I too have felt pain." We can be with the other only when the other ceases to be "other" and becomes like us (Nouwen, 1994, p. 105).

Authentic service comes from a deep compassion. And that deep compassion comes from being willing to touch our own fears, our own struggles, and our own pain and admit our need. When we do this, it is easier to respond to the need of another with very little calculation.

TRUE SERVICE IS THE BY-PRODUCT OF A CHANGED HEART, RATHER THAN THE PATH TO ACCEPTANCE.

We know what it is like to need help and to hope that someone will respond. This understanding or knowledge can protect us from thinking that it is the act of service that changes things. It is not the good deed but rather the connection with another, reflecting the love God has extended to us that makes the difference. Our sin grows from mistrust, fear, and insecurity. In the loving embrace of friend, family, priest, or acquaintance we remember that there is something beyond us that is at work and responds to our deepest need. True service is a natural response to another human being whom you choose to care about, rather than a path to prove your worth. It is the by-product of a changed heart, rather than the path to acceptance.

That is why relationship is so important to the authentic service that forms our identities and spirits. True service is a response to another's need, rather than the demonstration of my purpose. When I do good to others with the motive of bettering myself, I am exploitive. I give, but do so with little regard for the person to whom I give. In an exploitive gift, any needy person will do. I need to give because I want to, or I believe I need to, or it is my duty. I just need to find a cause and give myself to it. That is a very different action than responding to someone who is in front of me. What I do is determined by what is really going to be helpful to the other, even if it makes me feel useless, powerless, and small. What does that mean?

GIVING INSIDE THE BOUNDS OF RELATIONSHIP KEEPS ME HONEST.

> *When I reflect on my own life, I realize that the moments of greatest comfort and consolation were moments when someone said: "I cannot take your pain away, I cannot offer you a solution for your problem, but I can promise you that I won't leave you alone and will hold on to you as long and as well as I can"* (NOUWEN, 1994, P. 105).

Relationship provides a protective coating around our motives. To be sure, we may never completely remove the taint of human ambition. I give because it feels good. But giving inside the bounds of relationship keeps me honest. We cannot hide from our motives and intentions when the person across from us knows us.

Finally, this relationship focus will ask me to learn from people I never thought could teach me. There is a reason that the Scriptures tend to push us to spend time around the poor. They have much to teach us if we will listen. The poor, who live with sharply limited resources, do not rely on the artificial props of possessions, status, image, or accolades to make themselves feel valued. All the poor have is that which they can give for little or no cost. Those are things of relationship—kindness, stories, a helping hand, and a shared hope. I am constantly amazed when I go to the poorest of places by how happy and well-adjusted people tend to be. The poor life is not to be romanticized. It is difficult, and any one of the poor would take an easier lot in life. Yet they remind me that what I think I need to be okay is really unnecessary. I do not need an upwardly mobile career to be important. I do not need power to be helpful. The simplicity in the life of the poor is just like the simplicity of the trail for the pilgrim. It challenges the illusions that affluence fosters.

The relationship focus will ask me to learn from people I never thought could teach me.

I have made many trips to Mexico on various cross-cultural service projects. There are two incidents that stick out in my mind most clearly. They both happened on the same trip to the town of Creel in Chihuahua, Mexico. We were there helping a small church that lacked even running water. We met in a small, plain room warmed by an old wooden stove in the corner. During our stay, the pastor was away, delayed on a trip, so his wife took responsibility for the meeting. In that last chair in the last row on the left-hand side of the room sat a drunk. I think he chose the seat because it was closest to the stove. He clearly had been well "watered" before coming to the church. He sat in the back and slept as his head bobbed and weaved like a punch-drunk boxer. He paid no attention, apparently, to what we were doing. After the meeting, we had lunch at the church. The pastor's wife fixed our guest a plate and woke him in order to feed him. What made the act of charity genuine in my mind was that she required nothing in return. She did not do it to create a sense of debt that could be paid back by joining the church and straightening up his life. No, she simply gave food to a hungry man who could not feed himself.

Later that week, our small group was invited to the home of a church member for dinner. This night was a big deal for our host. She spared no expense in extending her hospitality to us. We were told that our entree for the night was a real treat—a meal rarely experienced by this family. When she brought out the dish and removed the lid, we looked down upon this delicacy. What looked back at us was a pot of green beans. I had traveled hundreds of miles from the United States to help the poor only to be taught by the genuine kindness of our host to see the small things as the most important.

The lessons of authentic, spirit-forming service are not easily learned. The disciples walked every day for 3 years with the Master of compassionate service. And yet, even at the end, they still had not learned the lesson. They were still too dedicated to proving their own worth and value. Peter would not have his feet washed.* On the surface, this may have seemed an act of humility, and a lesser teacher might have been fooled. Jesus saw it for what it was. It was the resistant act of a proud man who did not realize that the path to life is paved with our limitations rather than our strengths. Peter, like us, did not fully understand the depth of our need to protect ourselves from our weaknesses. The containers we have outlined for spiritual formation do for us what Jesus' foot-washing ritual did for Peter. They bring us to a place of awareness and attention where we can see both who we truly are and the depth of God's commitment to us.

---

*John 13:1-11

9 Containers Applied

In this section, I want to discuss some practical matters. How do we use the containers of retreat, pilgrimage, and service to promote learning? In my experience, I always used a combination of containers. What I want to do here is to provide some ideas for what they could look like and did look like in my work in hopes that your own thinking will be stimulated. How do we create the containers of retreat, pilgrimage, and service in the real world? In my experience, rarely did I use a pure form of the containers. It was always a combination of containers. These are not the only form these containers can take, nor will I be exhaustive in writing about how to do each one. What I want to do is to provide some ideas for what they could look like and did look like in my work.

How do we create the containers of retreat, pilgrimage, and service in the real world?

Service and Pilgrimage – Short-Term Missions

I step across the border crossing and I have a very perceptible release of tension. I am once again in my home country, though things are not so different just a few miles across the border. This happens to me each time I go on a short-term mission. After almost a dozen trips out of the U.S., I still feel the same response. This tells me that my time on mission has a real and deep impression upon me. It has been a container that has caused me to change pace, endure the unknown, and give to something other than my own interests. What exactly, though, does the cross-cultural mission experience do to help form our spirits? I can only talk about what it has done for me.

My first mission trip was my senior year of high school when our youth group went to Monterrey, Mexico. Later, I would be responsible for leading 80 to 90 college students to the state of Chihuahua, Mexico. I have been in Mexico's big cities and some of the most remote areas in North America. I worked with the rich, the poor, and the middle class. I helped build buildings, spoke in open meetings, and lived with the locals. But what has this experience done to me?

First of all, I gained some notion of what it means to be a pilgrim—a stranger in the land. Mexicans are very warm and welcoming people. Yet, no amount of hospitality can remove the fact that I did not speak the language, and I did not know their history. In spite of all the similarities, I was unaccustomed to their rules. Being a stranger has a double effect. It makes you self-conscious about what you do, what you believe, and the nature of your own culture and how you find your place in it. It also makes you pay close attention to everything that goes on around you. How people eat, when they eat, what they eat, how they talk, how they sit, how they work, how they use the restroom—these are things I would not give a second thought about in my own country, and yet they are of such consequence in a foreign land. This heightened inward and outward attention is good training for learning to watch and wait in order to discern what God is doing in the world around us. I never take the lead in a foreign land and neither should we take the lead in spiritual formation. It is always a response that comes out of following the lead of the ones who know best.

I never take the lead in a foreign land and neither should we take the lead in spiritual formation.

A second work of mission trips is that they make us stop and rethink our assumptions about helping others. Unfortunately, too many people believe mission trips are about bringing "God to the heathen." It has been my experience that this assumption could be very false. God is always at work in all peoples. He has always been so, even from ancient times. Even though we go to offer help and resources to those with less financial resources, it is often the poor who have the better lessons to teach. The happiness of the poor is often based on relationships rather than activity or possessions. They give freely of what they have—friendship,

Even though we go to offer help and resources to those with less financial resources, it is often the poor who have the better lessons to teach.

support, care, and concern. They make those of us who are more affluent stop and listen differently. There is gratitude for the smallest things. This too is important for the work of spiritual formation. The steps we take to live into an experienced faith are small and progress is often imperceptible. Yet, we must trust that it is happening. Occasionally we see obvious forward movement, but for me, learning to appreciate the small things has been very important. The world is changed through the collective effect of small changes.

Perhaps the best way to summarize the lessons of cross-cultural trips is that they allow us to experience being lost. It is a form of sacrifice in terms of giving up what we know, control, and do in order to go to a place where we do not know the customs, the language, the geography, or the history. We don't know what to do to be productive. If we pay attention to the poverty we brush against, we will feel overwhelmed at how big a problem it is. It is being lost that grows our faith more than any amount of goodness. "When we engage in an act of faith we give up control, we give up sensory confirmation of reality (sight, hearing, etc.); we give up insisting on head-knowledge as our primary means of orientation in life" (Peterson, 2007, p. 44). Leaving is the disturbance that leads to the chaos of being lost, which brings us to letting go of illusions that allow us to reorient our lives once again toward an identity formed around God's provisions and actions for us.

Retreat and Pilgrimage – Wilderness Excursion

The strap, which had a deficit of padding, cut into my shoulder and left me wondering if it would not just continue to pass right through my body. The burden on my back crushed me with each step leaving me to believe that I would never be right again. I went to sleep in a tent pitched in the black hole of the night. I went to bed tired, hurt, and disoriented only to awake from my ritual death of sleep to rejuvenation and a recovery of my senses and place. This is just a few thoughts that I still carry with me from my 14-day wilderness excursion. I spent 2 weeks navigating over 100 miles of northern Michigan and Wisconsin on the adventure that I took with HoneyRock (HoneyRock Northwoods Camp and Campus of Wheaton College). It was the hardest thing I have ever done, but it taught me lessons that I might never have learned otherwise.

Wilderness excursion is a combination of retreat and pilgrimage. These trips slow the pace of life to a crawl. There is plenty of time for thought and introspection. And there is just as much time for that thought to take hold. If the trip is longer than just a couple of days, we will not possibly be able to run from the lessons that are seeking to encroach on us. The limitations that appear continue to appear until we pay attention. The pain that we feel continues to betray the doubt and fear that secretly lies in wait within us all. We cannot run from ourselves or others in this context. The thoughts and introspection simply invade our consciousness until we start asking different questions. That is an element of retreat.

At the same time we are coming to grips with who we are, we find ourselves traipsing across an unknown land with an ambiguous destination. We might see the name or coordinates on our map, but we have no experience with what that destination really is. So we are motivated and enticed each day by the possibility of what might be found if we do reach the end.

Each day, I learn to leave behind what I think I know to awake to just a bit more awareness of my true position with God.

For me, one of the most important lessons that I learned was to trust dying or at least letting go. I would push my body to beyond what I believed it could do. I would crash into my sleeping bag, knowing that I would not be able to move the next day. Yet each day, as I trusted the artificial death that we experience as sleep, I would be resurrected a new person in the morning. I now see this as a sacrament of what is happening day after day in my spiritual walk. Each day, I learn to leave behind what I think I know to awake to just a bit more awareness of my true position with God. This growth of faith is a slow, long-term effort. It is difficult to trust in the beginning, just as I was surprised each morning on the trail, but I wake to a new start each morning.

Retreat – Project LIFE

In the early '90s, I was a youth pastor and we started an after-school adventure program that we call Project LIFE. LIFE was an acronym for Learning to Interact with Friends Effectively. The acronym never really caught on and we just went with Project Life. I started this program because I had a group of 11 and 12 year olds who were too old for children's choir and too young for the youth group. The basic structure of the program was that the kids came to the church once a week after school, played a warm-up game, got a snack, and took part in a teaching initiative (a problem-solving activity that required them to work together to accomplish a task). Twice a year we did a wilderness backpacking trip that included rock climbing, caving, and other adventurous activities. The kids were taught how to set up their own shelters, cook their own meals, and purify their own water. They were given the responsibility of navigating to our camp sites with a map and compass. In this program they learned who they were and how to ask the kinds of questions that would likely help them come into contact with what God was doing in their lives.

This was perhaps not the typical retreat context. After all, they came to the church building right after school. There was no long drive or secluded location for most of our time together. Yet, I think it had some of the basic elements of good retreat. To begin with, there was a change of pace for these kids when they came to Life. It was not a time dedicated to their entertainment and yet they did enjoy themselves. It was a time for them to take real and important roles for each other. Although there was action and activity, there was just as much emphasis on reflection, consideration, confession, and forgiveness. Now you might say, where did confession and forgiveness come from? When a group of people try to accomplish something, there are always mistakes. We focused on helping all participants to see their part in what had happened, to own their actions, and to ask for help from others to try new things in response to past mistakes. That is essentially the cycle of repentance that leads to a growing spirit. It was this mindset that we sought to practice and grow comfortable with.

Ultimately, this retreat setting was concerned with helping youth learn to ask meaningful questions and to wait and listen for answers. As a leader, I found myself amazed at how well they learned to do this on their own. As a spiritual facilitator, that is what you hope for. Can people I work with come away, not with everything figured out, but with the courage and commitment to ask important questions? If the answer is yes, it is only a matter of time until God bumps into them in a meaningful and life-changing way.

10 What Now?

There is one more question to consider. What now? How does the idea of experiential spiritual formation become a lived reality rather than just an interesting topic? I want to offer some suggestions for you to consider as you move toward the work of spiritual formation. There are some questions that you can first ask of yourself in order to understand your own faith and identity. We cannot help others find what is still lost to us. Secondly, there are questions that you can use to evaluate the methods and means that you are using in your ministry and work with others right now. And finally, I will offer a framework for you to consider as you become more intentional in inviting others to participate in learning experiences.

Personal Reflection

1. Thinking back in your life, what stories were you drawn to? What does that tell you about what you believe about yourself and your assumptions about life?

Example: As a child, I loved superhero stories. I was always intrigued by stories whose characters had something special about them that set them apart from others. To this day, I am drawn to the genre of fantasy novels where some unsuspecting person finds his way into a journey of great purpose and along the way discovers that he has a special ability that will help others. Along with the newly discovered powers is often a struggle to know how he fits in and how he lives with the secret of who he really is.

Lessons about me: I know that I wonder if people would really like me if they knew me. I also tend to believe that if I could do something spectacular, that would relieve my self-doubt and provide me security. Consequently, I am continuously tempted to do something great in the hopes of finding a place to belong. The illusion that haunts me is that if I can produce, then I will be more valuable.

2. What do you fear most?

3. What do you believe makes you valuable?

4. What would be different about your leadership if you could let go of trying to be in control?

5. When you need real support and guidance, who do you talk to and why?

6. What has been your greatest adventure? What made it a great adventure?

7. Who is at the center of the story in your life, God and His actions or you and your actions?

8. What questions are you still asking?

9. What doubts still sneak up on you?

A sample from my journal may illustrate the nature of this question:

As I sat reading the book *The Shack*, I realized a subtle jealousy because I have not ever written anything so creative. The author attributes the book's success to it being a "God thing." Why does God bless his work and not mine? *Is there something unacceptable about me?* It is appropriate on this my 43rd birthday that I come once again in contact with the question I have and will pursue my entire life. I do not know if I will ever find the answer, but at least the question is framed. I started thinking about all the rejections I have faced, and I realized that what continues to drive me (though to a lesser degree now) is the need to do something successful because I question my value. In the book, God is talking to Mack and He says, "Trust is the fruit of a relationship in which you know you are loved. Because you do not know that I love you, you cannot trust me" (p. 126).

> In my life, I would change this statement to say, "Contentment is the fruit of a relationship in which you know you are important. Because you do not know that God values you and your life, you are never content. In fact, you are always drawn to things that ring of changing the world, reforming the church, or starting a movement. You are not sure you can make yourself believe the truth." Knowing the truth is something that one must live into but one can choose to not believe a lie. Consequently, changing the world or being wildly successful will never give you the answer to the question, "Am I important?" I hope someday that I can live into the truth of that answer—yes, I am important, and so are we all.

10. What assumptions of yours are being challenged or revealed as you read this book?

11. Which of these leadership temptations are hardest for you?

    - Being relevant
    - Being spectacular
    - Being powerful
    - Being in control
    - Coming to the rescue
    - Proving your worth
    - Being productive

• Work or Leadership Reflections

1. What are you currently trying to get your students to do or believe?

2. Do you provide more answers or questions to those you disciple?

3. What percentage of the time with your students do you spend talking about their stories and experiences versus talking about stories of others?

4. What has been your best experience with a group? What made it so great?

5. What has been your worst group experience? What made it bad?

6. What kinds of experiences do you give your students now? What is the purpose of those experiences?

7. How often do your students reveal their failures, fears, and limitations? Why do you think that is?

8. If you could get your students to ask different or better questions, which questions would you want them to ask?

9. What conditions could you change or create that would better promote spiritual formation and authentic community?

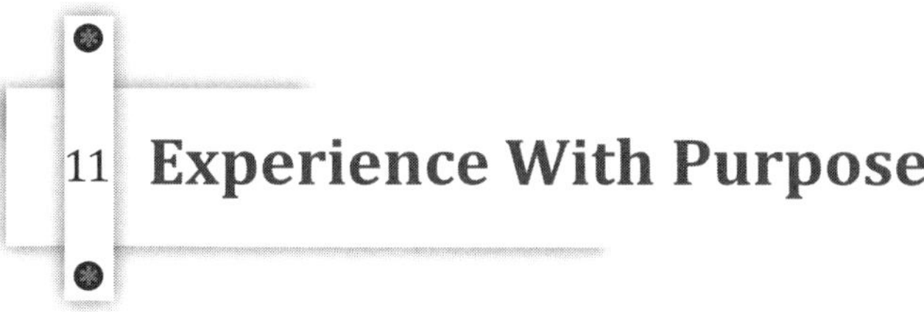

11 Experience With Purpose

In Daniel Quinn's book *Beyond Civilization* (1999) he says, "If the world is to be changed it will not be with old minds with new programs but with new minds with no programs at all." So I must confess I write this section with great trepidation, for I do not want to leave the impression that we can somehow program spiritual formation or make faith happen in the lives of those we lead. Many of the metaphors about how faith comes about in our lives speak of trees and fruit. Trees naturally bear fruit and there is nothing we can do to make that happen faster. Yet, I realize the pragmatic truth that to walk alongside others in this day and time will require us to structure some experiences so that we can increase our encounters with others. With this in mind, I want to provide a way of thinking about how to organize our learning experiences so that they might build on one another.

Events With Purpose

We have the opportunity to not only create successful events but to also pass on the abilities and practices that will enable the search for truth and faith over a lifetime. Taking this long-term view of faith development will help us structure experiences that build upon one another. Here are a few examples.

Reflection: In order for us to see the things that God is doing in our lives, we must connect to our own experience. An experiential approach to spiritual formation will help people come back to and tell their own stories. This approach sees the experience of a person as the starting point for all learning. What do I mean by this? If we learn to listen to and reflect on our lives and the lives of those in our immediate community, the questions that we need to consider and the particular truths that we need to understand will be revealed. Rather than teach from a prescribed lesson plan, the spiritual facilitator begins with his or her participants' current experiences and then uses Scripture and truth to help the participants make sense of their lives and the experience. It is a way of teaching that depends more on questions than answers, and the intent is to help those we work with learn to ask their own questions.

> THE EXPERIENCE OF A PERSON IS THE STARTING POINT FOR ALL LEARNING.

Prayer: In reflection we are listening to our own lives; in prayer we are listening to God. Now the most common form of prayer is a speech we make to God asking for things. This is not the type of prayer that is of the most importance. It is important that we learn to orient our lives to turn to God first when we need support and clarity. Jesus called us to obedience.[*] The word "obedience" means to listen. A life of prayer and obedience is not a life that learns a set of rules and then keeps those rules so that their requests have a better chance of being granted. A life of prayer makes space to listen for the voice of God in whatever form it might come to us. It is the type of life where we let go of our need to know all the answers. We let go of rushing to God so that our own discomfort is relieved. We learn to trust and wait for Truth to find us and help us see our way forward.

> WE LEARN TO TRUST AND WAIT FOR TRUTH TO FIND US AND HELP US SEE OUR WAY FORWARD.

Honesty: This idea goes back to our chapter on community. We must be willing to tell ourselves the truth and to hear the truth of others, without needing to fix them. Authenticity and the courage to see both our strengths and our limitations is important if we want true community with mature individuals. We must learn to talk about the fears, failures, and facades that we use to protect ourselves. In these things hide the assumptions that we must challenge as God brings us to a clearer understanding of who He sees us to be.

Openness: One of the ways that we clarify our own assumptions is to encounter the perspectives and stories of others. When we listen to others with respect and openness, we accomplish a couple

---

[*] John 14:15, 21

of things. First, we will hear things that may be different than what we have experienced or thought. In contacting these differences, we will be forced to clarify our own beliefs as we evaluate the perspectives of others. Secondly, if we are open to others, we will come into contact with new and different questions that we could never have thought of on our own. This may be because the people we interact with come from a different place, culture, or time, but in their questions, we discover questions that we could not give voice to or ones that we never even considered asking. I know that in the last church that I worked at, every 3 months we would bring our senior citizens together with our high school students. We would often watch a movie and discuss it. The point was to bring generations separated by decades together believing that each would stimulate the other to consider new ideas and questions. Spiritual formation is personal but not an individual work. We need a community to help us see what we cannot see on our own.

SPIRITUAL FORMATION IS PERSONAL BUT NOT AN INDIVIDUAL WORK.

Put the Right Character at the Center of the Story: Although as spiritual facilitators we do not have the power to grow the spirits or faith of those we work with, we can help in the process by continuing to remind people that God is at the center of all the stories. When we get away from spiritual formation and wander back into a life of being good, right, and productive, we focus more on what we do than what God is and has done on our behalf. We must consistently return to the truth of Jesus' acceptance of us each time we talk together. It is God's reconciliation with all things, His making things right between us, that anchors a life of faith. It is at the root of our true identity and is the revelation of our true value. When we keep the right character at the center of the story, we can find our way amid the variety of voices trying to tell us who we are and how to be. This understanding is essential for my students as well as myself.

WE MUST CONSISTENTLY RETURN TO THE TRUTH OF JESUS' ACCEPTANCE OF US EACH TIME WE TALK TOGETHER.

Sequencing of Events

Leaders have responsibility for more than an individual event; they need an approach or program to work with students over time. I want to provide a model that might help leaders think about the types of experiences they organize and the purpose of those experiences.

Ideally, experiences are structured so that interested individuals will be challenged more, exposed to deeper issues, and have the opportunity to take up roles of escalating responsibility and leadership. With this in mind, I offer this four-level model, which includes Awareness, Immersion, Mastery, and Regeneration. Figure 10.1 (p. 95) provides an overview of the model. This model can be looked at as a macrocycle in which participants are led from awareness to regeneration over a long period of time (i.e., a 3- to 4-year process). It can also be used as a micro-cycle with participants completing the cycle in a year, moving on to new and more challenging experiences each year.

Awareness is where we begin. Learning and spiritual formation are processes that typically start with a growing awareness and recognition of things not noticed or experienced before. The awareness phase is designed to introduce participants to

1) a new medium of learning (type of experience) and
2) to new ideas and questions.

These typically are experiences that are short in duration and aim to create confidence in that particular activity or experience as well as generate the desire to learn more about a subject or question. An awareness-building experience is successful if those who participate leave wanting more of that type of activity and having new questions to consider. In fact, the better the awareness-building experience, the greater the number of questions and the fewer answers. Answers will come. I remember when I was in college, we had a speaker come in for a series of lectures in chapel. His subject was something that I had no exposure to in my past. At the end of the week, I remember realizing that I had just experienced something very important to my spiritual formation but I had no idea what that was. I had burning questions with few answers. This led me to start a deeper search for answers to questions that gained clarity as I searched. That is an ideal awareness-building experience.

A BETTER AWARENESS-BUILDING EXPERIENCE RESULTS IN MORE QUESTIONS THAN ANSWERS.

Once an interest has been created, move onto **Immersion** experiences. Immersion experiences are much longer in duration and have as goals

1) the development of specific skills, attitudes, and abilities and

2) a community of learners who become proficient at learning from and with each other.

> Immersion is where participants will begin to find some of the answers to their questions.

Immersion is where participants will begin to find some of the answers to their questions. It is the level of experience where we try to instill the attitudes and skills described earlier in this chapter under the "Events with a Purpose" heading.

For example, let's return to Project Life, the after-school adventure program that I ran years ago for middle school students. My core goals were helping kids learn to reflect on their experience (e.g., asking questions, slowing down so they could look back), develop trust and respect for others in their Life groups, and develop confidence and willingness to take responsibility for themselves. That is an Immersion experience.

Once participants are equipped with skill, attitude, and confidence, they are ready to move on to **Mastery**. I want to provide a clear warning here. Mastery does not mean having a complete set of answers nor does it indicate perfection. We never really complete mastery of most things, especially spiritual formation. But we can develop a level of experience and confidence that enables us to apply what we have learned in novel settings, or with a different group of people. Mastery is a stage of new exploration that has higher expectations and greater challenges than an Awareness experience. The goals of Mastery are

> Mastery does not mean having a complete set of answers nor does it indicate perfection.

1) to apply skills and abilities in new settings and

2) to deepen the ability of participants to assess and change themselves.

Ultimately, a person who has completed Mastery-level experiences has a broader experience and is equipped to perpetuate his or her own learning and development outside any program or teacher.

For example, a group of junior high students has been participating for a while in local adventure experiences like challenge course or backpacking. As they move into high school, these students may want to take on an extreme mission project with both adventure activities and the opportunity to invest in a poor community in another country. This type of experience will escalate the depth of questions for participants and will allow them to apply their experiential and collective learning skills in a very new setting.

Finally, participants are ready to take on the development of the next generation of learners. In the **Regeneration** stage, participants become teachers and mentors for others. The goals of this stage are

1) to pass on to others an enthusiasm for learning and searching for the truth and
2) to continue to mature as a person while facilitating learning with others.

The truth is that we never cease to be the student, the learner, the disciple that God is forming, but we do reach a time when our journey can help inform the journey of others. This is when we get to participate in the work God is doing in the life of another. We can help God-seekers come into contact with new questions, our questions, which can help them on their own path to maturity, mastery, and regeneration. I know that my own growth was helped by friends, spiritual facilitators, who invested their time with me. Through the life they lived, they helped me ask different questions, look for new answers, and come to see who I was and could become.

> MY OWN GROWTH WAS HELPED BY FRIENDS, SPIRITUAL FACILITATORS, WHO INVESTED THEIR TIME WITH ME.

Figure 10.2 (p. 96) outlines a sample of how this might work in a youth ministry setting. There are many different ways this can be applied. What starts as a pre-teen, single-day adventure outing could progress to participation in an after-school adventure program, where students find out who they are and how to learn from experience. They can then proceed to new settings where they learn in different ways and may even take the lead in some aspect of the community's activities together. Finally, those students who wish to do so become teachers and mentors for the generation following behind them.

Figure 10.3 (p. 97) looks at this progression, not as the macro sequence over a number of years but as a mini sequence that grows in intensity, complexity, and challenge each year. So on some small scale, students pass from awareness to mastery of a particular type of experience over 1 year. The next year they start again with awareness but at a deeper level than the previous year. For instance, in the area of missionary work, an awareness-building activity is a local work project that leads to a short-term missions project where a person may go to another country for a week or two to do a service project. The next year, that person could start with a short-term project in a new country or setting that ends with a longer trip, a couple of months, where he or she starts to learn a new language. The next year, that person might start an intermediate level trip, spending 1 to 2 years in another country or take on leadership responsibilities for additional short-term trips. Finally, that person might become a career missionary or begin to lead trips for others.

Developing the practices and mindset that promote spiritual formation over a lifetime requires us to learn in a variety of settings and continue to deepen our commitment to searching out the truth. As facilitators we can help people continue to stretch their thinking and faith when we introduce novel containers and environments where we help people contact new questions and perspectives. Our best effort is to not just continue with random activities in which we hope the necessary lessons stick. Although we cannot program spiritual formation, we can be purposeful in providing opportunities that build both in terms of intensity, skill set, and sophistication as well as parallel the ongoing maturing of those with whom we work.

Sequencing of Events

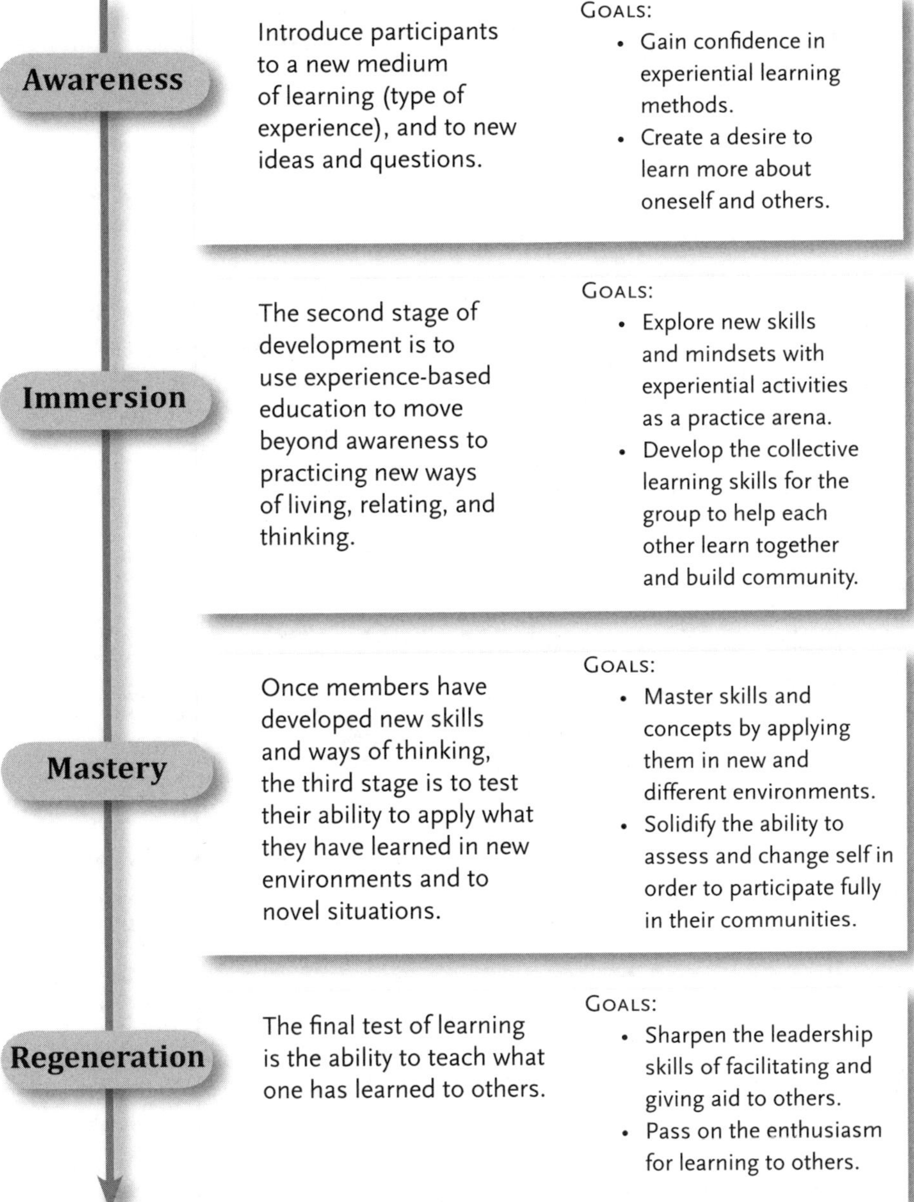

Figure 10.1

Sample Plan - Layered Learning Experiences

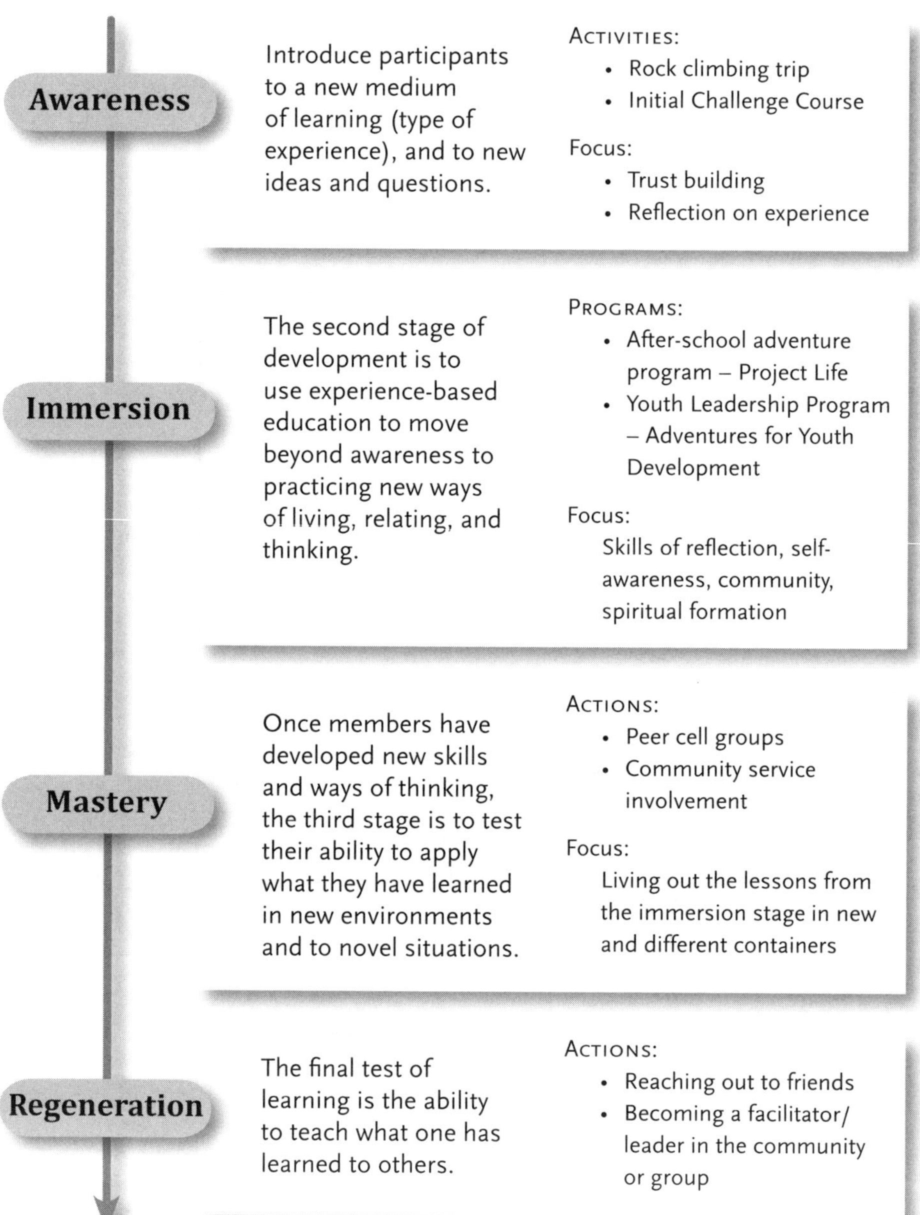

Figure 10.2

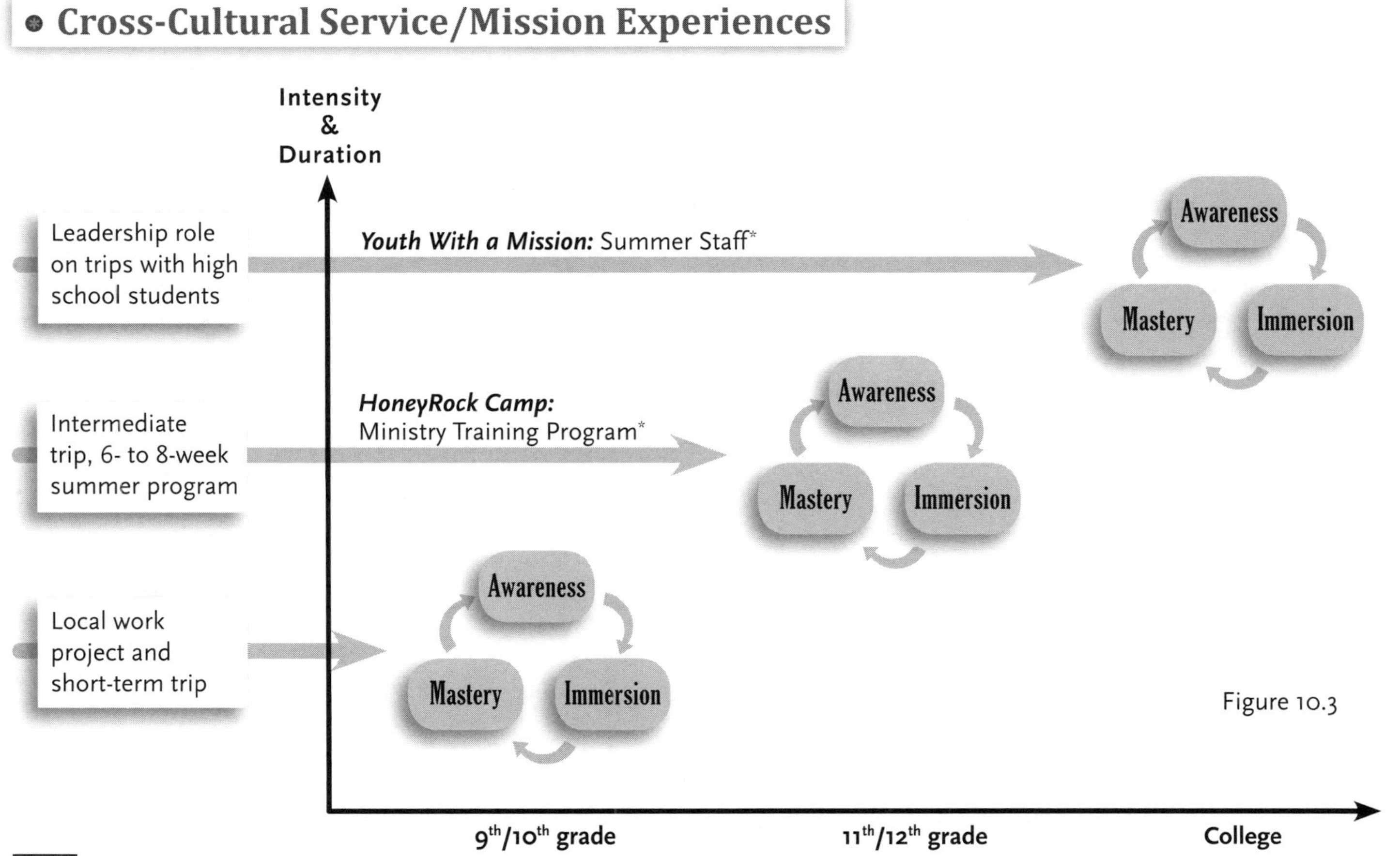

Figure 10.3

* See program descriptions in Appendix, p. 101.

If the world is to be changed it will not be with old minds with new programs but with new minds with no programs at all.

—Daniel Quinn

Final Thoughts

Spiritual facilitators walk along a fine line. On one hand, spiritual formation is truly a work done by God in our lives. On the other hand, we have the ability to be purposeful in helping others awaken to the spirit-oriented life that's available to them. If we overplan, we will put the wrong person(s) at the center of the story. We will imply that spiritual formation, faith building, can be programmed. We will look to formulas with predictable outcomes rather than entering the mystery that is the life of faith. We will see those we help as charges we are responsible for changing and risk doing harm to those who do not walk at the pace we set.

We may find some protection by only teaching what we have experienced. If we commit to discovery and trust that God will work at the right time, we will not run too far in front. Rather, we will remain curious onlookers as we await our next opportunity to participate in God's work. We must hold tight to the idea that we are only companions on the journey of faith with those we come into community with. Finally, we must always be open to the truth that reveals both our wondrous gifts as well as our limitations. We must learn that even those limitations are not our shame to hide but gifts that keep us from wandering too far on our own.

Hospitality is not to change people, but to offer them space where change can take place. It is not to bring men and women over to our side, but to offer freedom not disturbed by dividing lines. It is not to lead our neighbor into a corner where there are no alternatives left, but to open a wide spectrum of options for choice and commitment.

—Henri Nouwen

Appendix

Program Descriptions from Figure 10.3 (p. 97)

HoneyRock—Ministry Training Program

Ministry Training Program (Grades 10-12)
This program is for high school students who are ready to take it to the next level and learn how to serve Christ with their whole lives. During the first 3 weeks of MTP, students will spend some time at HoneyRock becoming a team through a variety of challenge course experiences. The team will then depart in vans for a 2-week wilderness expedition to Canada. After spending a few days back at camp to pack and prepare, the team will then depart for Costa Rica where they will spend 2 weeks on a missions trip bringing fresh, clean water to some villages in need. HoneyRock has partnered with LeaderTreks, an organization specializing in youth missions trips overseas, to organize and help lead this trip. The final few days will be spent back at HoneyRock debriefing the experience and preparing for life back home. MTP is for high schoolers who have completed Advance Camp, DTP, Service Team, or another intense youth ministry program and meet the criteria for acceptance into the program. A special application is necessary for all participants; this will be sent to you when we receive your registration. Passport required.

Costa Rica Trip Details
HoneyRock has a special partnership with LeaderTreks (Carol Stream, IL) to coordinate and help lead this missions trip experience for MTP participants. LeaderTreks has over 12 years' experience leading youth missions trips and other leadership development adventures throughout the world. They have been working in Costa Rica for over 3 years and have full-time missionary staff, who are Wheaton College alumni, that live and work in Costa Rica year-round. LeaderTreks is a premier organization with highly qualified, professional leaders who, partnered with HoneyRock's staff, will ensure a safe and life-changing trip for students. HoneyRock is very confident that working with LeaderTreks ensures the right experience, resources, and staff to provide this opportunity for our campers.

Overview: Guanacaste is located in the northwest region of Costa Rica. It is a beautiful and often overlooked region in Costa Rica. Scattered throughout the mountains are small villages whose people live in a more primitive way. They are without many of the resources that you and I could never imagine missing—clean water, education, or even a church building. MTP will work with remote village churches to help bring fresh water to their communities. These sites rarely have any visitors from the developed world. We'll be working with people that no one else wants to help. We will be building water pipe systems to bring water right to where people live. Many of these communities have been overlooked by their own country, so imagine how powerful the message is of a team of high school students coming to serve them in the name of Jesus Christ.

(From HoneyRock website http://www.honeyrockcamp.org/storyGallery.asp?storyid=102)

Youth With A Mission

YWAM Explained

Youth With A Mission (YWAM) encompasses thousands of people and hundreds of ministries in almost every country of the world. In every case, our passion is to know God and to make Him known.

We are a mixture of people from all over the world, from 149 countries, in fact. In many of our locations, people from a wide variety of nations serve side by side. We come from numerous different Christian denominations and speak hundreds of languages. Nearly half of our staff come from "non-western" countries, such as Brazil, Korea, Indonesia, India, and Nepal.

We have a full-time staff, and many YWAM locations host short-term outreach teams made up of individuals, youth groups, families, and churches who get to participate firsthand in "making God known" through both words and actions. We send out over 25,000 short-term missionaries each year.

There are three strands of ministry weaving throughout all that YWAM does:

Evangelism: Some creative tools used to present the gospel include drama, music, performing arts, and sports camps. YWAMers want to effectively share their faith in ways that the audience—whether teenagers, elderly refugees, or an unreached people group—will understand. YWAM also engages in church planting among unreached people groups.

Mercy Ministry: Mercy Ministry is the "hands and feet" of making God known. YWAM helps meet some of the practical and physical needs of about 400,000 people annually. Caring for street children in South America; aiding in the recovery of drug addicts in North America and Western Europe; feeding and housing refugees and women in need in Africa and Asia; and operating ships that declare the good news practically and verbally are just some of the ways in which helping hands are extended.

Training and Discipleship: Training and Discipleship aim to better equip Christians to serve others in everything from agriculture and health care to drug rehabilitation and biblical counseling. Through YWAM's University of the Nations (U of N), missionaries can study in specialized areas such as science and technology, linguistics, the humanities, and Christian ministry. Most YWAM schools combine classroom teaching with relationship-centered discipleship and practical service. The Discipleship Training School (DTS) is a requirement for applying as YWAM staff and serves as a prerequisite to all other training programs. Each year some 10,000 students attend a U of N school at one of the 250 different locations.

Get Involved: If you're interested in exploring specific opportunities in YWAM, you can use the search function on the Web site to browse through YWAM locations, outreach trips, staff openings, volunteer opportunities, and even people groups that we work with. If you find something that interests you, you can find out about application procedures, costs, and other information by contacting that YWAM location directly. In YWAM, although we do have main offices, we encourage you to contact our field locations directly to explore opportunities to serve.

(From YWAM Web site http://www.ywam.org/contents/abo_wha_ywamexplained.htm)

• Resources

If you have been moved to pursue the ideas in this book in your own work, you may need some help. The following organizations are potential partners and places for additional training.

Challenge Quest, LLC
Training in adventure pursuits, challenge course, and spiritual facilitation
www.challengequest.com
info@challengequest.com

HoneyRock
Training in adventure pursuits, graduate and undergraduate courses, program partners for extended adventure/service experiences
www.honeyrockcamp.org
888-859-9525

Initiatives International
Partner for short-term mission experiences
www.initiativesinterational.org
877-535-1233

Tell Their Story
Partner for innovative, sustainable service projects in developing countries
www.telltheirstory.org
contact@telltheirstory.org

• References

Abdullah, S. (1999). *Creating a world that works for all.* San Fransicso: Berrett-Koehler Publishers.

Barry, W. A. (2001). *Letting God come close: An approach to Ignatian spiritual exercises.* Chicago: Loyola Press.

Boers, A. P. (2007). *The way is made by walking: A pilgrimage along the Camino De Santiago.* Downers Grove, IL: Intervarsity Press.

Capon, R. F. (1998). *The foolishness of preaching: Proclaiming the gospel against the wisdom of the world.* Grand Rapids, MI: William B. Eerdmans Publishing Company.

Cousins, N. (1981). *Human options, an autobiographical notebook.* New York: W W Norton.

Cron, I. M. (2006). *Chasing Francis: A pilgrim's tale.* Colorado Springs, CO: NavPress.

Dawn, M. J., Peterson, E. H. & Santucci, P. (2000). *The unnecessary pastor: Rediscovering the call.* Grand Rapids, MI: Wm. B. Eerdmans Publishing Co.

de Mello, A. (1990). *Awareness.* New York: Image Books.

Ewert, A. W. (1989). *Outdoor adventure pursuits: Foundations, models and theories.* Scottsdale, AZ: Publishing Horizons, Inc.

Kruger, C. B. (2003). *Jesus and the undoing of Adam.* Jackson, MS: Perichoresis Press.

Nouwen, H. (1974). *Out of solitude: Three meditations on the Christian life.* Notre Dame, IN: Ave Maria Press.

Nouwen, H. (1975). *Reaching out.* New York: Doubleday.

Nouwen, H. (1981). *The way of the heart: Connecting with God through prayer, wisdom, and silence.* San Francisco: HarperSanFrancisco.

Nouwen, H. (1988). *The modern spirituality series: Henri Nouwen, 1988.* Springfield, IL: Templegate Publishers.

Nouwen, H. (1989). *In the name of Jesus: Reflections on Christian leadership.* New York: Crossroad.

Nouwen, H. (1994). *Here and now: Living in the spirit.* New York: Crossroad.

Nouwen, H. (2005). *Peacework: Prayer, resistance, community.* Maryknoll, NY: Orbis Books.

Nouwen, H. (2006). *Spiritual direction: Wisdom for the long walk of faith.* San Francisco: HarperSanFrancisco.

Palmer, P. J. (1990). *The active life: A spirituality of work, creativity, and caring.* San Francisco: HarperSanFrancisco.

Palmer, P. J. (2000). *Let your life speak.* San Francisco: Jossey Bass.

Peterson, E. H. (2003). *The Message: The Bible in contemporary language.* Colorado Springs, CO: NavPress.

Peterson, E. H. (2005). *Christ plays in ten thousand places: A conversation in spiritual theology.* Grand Rapids, MI: Eerdmans Publishing Company.

Peterson, E. H. (2007). *The Jesus way: A conversation on the ways that Jesus is the way.* Grand Rapids, MI: Wm. B. Eerdmans Publishing Co.

Quinn, D. (1999). *Beyond civilization: Humanity's next great adventure.* New York: Random House, Inc.

Robinson, G. & Rose, M. (2006). *A leadership paradox: Influencing others by defining yourself, Rev Ed.* Bloomington, IN: Authorhouse.

Silf, M. (1999). *Inner compass: An invitation to Ignatian spirituality.* Chicago: Loyola Press.

Strong, J. (1977). *Strong's exhaustive concordance, student edition.* Grand Rapids, MI: Baker Book House.

Taylor, D. (2005). *In search of sacred places: Looking for wisdom on Celtic holy islands.* Saint Paul, MN: Bog Walk Press.

Walters, K. (2001). *Soul wilderness: A desert spirituality.* New York: Paulist Press.

About the Author

Greg Robinson is currently president of Challenge Quest, LLC in Pryor, Oklahoma. Previous to coming to Challenge Quest, Greg spent 5 years with Williams in Tulsa, Oklahoma as a managing organization development consultant. He also was the coordinator of experiential training at John Brown University. His professional career also included 10 years of youth ministry and 4 years of college ministry.

Greg has a PhD in Organizational Behavior and Leadership from The Union Institute and University in Cincinnati, Ohio. He also has an MS in Counseling from John Brown University.

Greg's professional career has concentrated in the areas of team development, leadership development, and facilitation and consulting with organizational change efforts. He has coauthored three books with Mark Rose: *Teams for a New Generation: An Introduction to Collective Learning*; *A Leadership Paradox: Influencing Others by Defining Yourself;* and their newest book, *Teams for a New Generation: A Facilitator's Field Guide.*

Greg currently resides with his wife Jeannie, his daughter Keely, and son Kobe in Pryor, Oklahoma.

If you are interested in having Greg speak, lead a retreat, or give a workshop for your organization you can contact him at:

Greg@challengequest.com or 918-639-1676

Notes

● Notes